# CALIFORNIA'S HAUNTED ROUTE 66

## BRIAN CLUNE

Haunted America

Published by Haunted America
A Division of The History Press
Charleston, SC
www.historypress.com

*Unless otherwise noted, images are from the collection of Terri Clune.*

First published 2022

Manufactured in the United States

ISBN 9781467152426

Library of Congress Control Number: 2022937930

Historic Route 66 has become a worldwide travel phenomenon, with folks coming from all parts of the globe to drive its miles.

*This book is dedicated to all of the folks who strive day and night to keep the Mother Road alive for future generations so they can learn about America of the past, its struggles, growing pains and how much this historic roadway meant for the growth of the United States, into the beacon of freedom the country is today. This book is also dedicated to those who drive Route 66 and keep it surviving with their patronage and support.*

*Finally, I dedicate this to the woman I love, who, I believe may just be a witch, considering how much I love her, lol. I thank you all!*

*Anticipation. In love and travel, getting there is half the fun. The lustful impatience, the passionate daydreams, the nerve-wracking waiting…lovers and travelers are all alike when they find themselves on the brink of a new adventure.*

—*Vivian Swift,* Le Road Trip: A Traveler's Journal of Love and France

The Mojave Desert is one of the most inhospitable places in the country; despite the harsh environment, folks built towns and live under the hot desert sun.

# CONTENTS

# FOREWORD

As a devoted road tripper, I know how important it is to have a good map—or GPS these days—when you hop in the car and begin a journey! Route 66, also known as the Mother Road, is the ultimate road trip enjoyed by travelers who love history and the opportunity to stop and photograph memories for the future. And during this one-of-a-kind travel adventure, one may encounter memories or spirits from the past. Yes! Route 66 is one of the top haunted highways in the nation.

Having completed several sections of Route 66's 2,448 miles of highway—including the 285 miles in my book *Arizona's Haunted Route 66*—I know it takes a certain kind of person to research the stories and legends associated with this special journey. Brian Clune is your guide throughout *California's Haunted Route 66* and has spent many days and hours exploring historic ghost towns, hotels, theaters, cemeteries, train depots and, ending at one's final destination (no pun intended), the spectacular view of the Pacific Ocean from the Santa Monica Pier.

Travel with Clune to historic haunted locations such as the Calico Ghost Town a mere three miles off Route 66. Once a productive silver mining camp, it is now one of the most visited rebuilt ghost towns along California's historic highways. Having researched the vicinity in his book *Ghosts and Legends of Calico* (The History Press, 2020), Brian Clune is somewhat of an authority on the area. Learn about the spirits who still linger in the hillsides. Heard of Knott's Berry Farm? Learn about the connection between Walter

Knott's work at Calico Ghost Town and the famous Knott's Berry Farm in Buena Park, California.

Wander through the monuments and grave markers in the majestic Hollywood Memorial Park (Hollywood Forever) cemetery. Founded in 1899 by the Hollywood Cemetery Association, it's still celebrated as the final resting place for many of the who's who of Hollywood's film industry. Take a virtual tour with Clune as he relates some of the tales of well-known "permanent residents" such as Judy Garland, Rudolph Valentino, Douglas Fairbanks, Clifton Webb and budding actress Virginia Rappe. With a celebrity ghost story around the corner of nearly every mausoleum, Clune shares these eternal legacies with readers who yearn for a bit of stargazing and the need to be within six feet of their favorite Hollywood idol.

Make a photo stop at the Santa Monica Pier, which has gained fame and title as Route 66's last stop—or final destination. Although the pier was not the original ending point, the Route 66 Alliance and the Pier Restorations Corporation dedicated the spot as "the end of the Trail" in 2009. Brian Clune explains why the popular pier is more or less filled with energies of the past. Shadowy figures of visitors to the pier, former amusement park employees, soldiers during wartime and various Route 66 vacationers of the past have made their mark at the final destination point.

California's Haunted Route 66 will always be one of America's popular vacation adventures. So, let Brian Clune be *your* private paranormal travel guide through the scenic 315 miles of California's Mother Road. The historic and haunted roadway will excite you and get you in the spirit for your next road trip! Pack your bags, fill the gas tank and head on down the road—the Mother Road—and don't forget to bring your copy of this book!

—Debe Branning, author of *Arizona's Haunted Route 66*

# ACKNOWLEDGEMENTS

First, as always, I need to thank my acquisitions editor, Laurie Krill. She still actually takes my calls, even though she knows I will monopolize her time with questions and ask for advice and all sorts of other inquiries. I would also like to thank Scott Piotrowski, president of the California Historic Route 66 Association. Without his help, I would have been forever lost trying to figure out the myriad alignments that zigzag across Los Angeles and San Bernardino Counties. Thank you, Scott. I need to thank Willie Flores, manager of the Mayan Bar and Grill. Willie took me on a grand tour of the Aztec Hotel, gave me many stories and treated me like an honored guest. I would also like to thank Louis Montero for going on a few adventures with me while writing this book; his company and friendship helped keep me going. There are so many others I met along the Mother Road that I could not possibly mention them all, but each and every one of them was willing to tell me their stories, histories and haunted tales of this amazing road, and I shall always be thankful to them. Lastly, I want to thank my wife for being my traveling companion, editor and photographer for the book.

# 1
# THE AMERICAN CAR CULTURE

*Everything in life is somewhere else, and you get there in a car.*
*—Elwyn White*

America may not have been the birthplace of the automobile, but when Henry Ford began building his Model T, motorized personal transportation would forever dominate the American landscape from that day forward. When the first Model T rolled out of Ford's Michigan auto plant, he had yet to create the first production line, but people lined up to purchase this cheap and dependable newfangled automobile. Even though Ransom Olds sold what looked like a motorized horse buggy for only $650, the tiller-steered, hard-wheeled auto was hard to operate and control. Even though the Olds buggy sold 5,508 units, its rudimentary design and sparse accommodations never caught on with the general public. Before the Model T, cars were bought by the wealthy as a status symbol and amusement rather than a way to get around. With gasoline not widely available and the expensive cost of the more comfortable "luxury" models, the horse was still the main source of locomotion for not only common folk but the rich and famous as well. Ford would change all that when, in 1913, he created the world's first assembly line. This significantly reduced cost and sped up output, and with the ease of operation and an enclosed cab, the Model T allowed the general public to own and operate automobiles.

By 1909, there were approximately 253 American automobile manufacturers, with Ford leading the pack. In 1908, William Durant founded General Motors and began what would become one of the biggest rivalries in corporate American history. With the United States' spread-out settlements, with scattered and sometimes isolated rural farms and towns, the need for automobiles was clear. With a seller's market growing, by 1927, when production of this iconic car was withdrawn, Ford had manufactured 15 million Model Ts and was selling its next icon, the Ford Model A. The Model T originally cost $825, but by the time it was withdrawn, the coupe sold for a mere $290. With America having a significantly higher per capita income compared with the European economy, the growth of motorized transportation in the early days was all but assured. By 1913, America had produced roughly 485,000 of the world's 607,000 automobiles and trucks, and America's love affair with the car was on its way.

By 1929, the other auto manufactures had adopted Ford's moving production line concept, but of the 253 manufacturers in 1909, only 44 remained. Even though there were still quite a few auto builders, 80 percent of cars and trucks in the country were being built by Ford, General Motors and Chrysler, which was founded in 1925 by Walter Maxwell. Because of these company's production and sales standards, their ability to withstand adversity would come to the fore when the United States, and the world, was plunged into economic turmoil as the 1930s dawned. When the stock markets crashed on Black Thursday, October 24, 1929, the world was plunged into what would come to be known as the Great Depression. As people lost their jobs, their bank accounts dried up and what little money they had went for the basic necessities of life; the automotive industry all but came to a standstill. The economic downturn caused well-known but underperforming car manufacturers like Nash, Studebaker and Hudson to go out of business. Even though Packard managed to hang on, it too collapsed after World War II. Ford, Chrysler and GM, having money in reserve before the bank industry collapsed, managed to hang on, and it was this, more than anything else, that garnered them the nickname the "Big Three."

The Great Depression, while not generating sales for the Big Three, didn't kill America's need or love for the car. With the passage of the Federal Road Act in 1916 and the Federal Highway Act in 1921, the country had begun building new roadways and improving others. These roads were now being used by families to travel around the country looking for work and cheaper living. One of these roads was the newly formed Route 66, which ran from Chicago to California, or what colloquially became known as the "Land of Milk and Honey." Life and economics make strange bedfellows, and

America's car culture has never waned, and its love of the automobile can be seen in many places along the Mother Road.

sometimes the things that can be the most devastating to our world can also have a beneficial side to them that we can't see or fathom at the time they are happening. When World War II began for Europe in 1939, it would be not only the most barbaric and destructive period in human existence but also the catalyst for economic recovery from the worst financial crisis in history.

For the United States, war began on December 7, 1941, and set into motion the largest economic and industrial revolution the world had ever known. As the "Arsenal of Democracy," America had already begun tooling up its weapons manufacturing for the Lend-Lease agreement between Allied nations and the United States, but when Pearl Harbor was attacked, the country built up its industrial power at a rate never before seen. U.S. car manufacturing was at the very heart of that production. GM, Ford, Chrysler and Packard stopped all production of automobiles and began manufacturing tanks, aircraft, munitions and parts for the same and, of course, military trucks and armored cars. The massive amount of equipment and vehicles required meant that people were needed on the production lines. Since American men were needed on the battlefields, across the oceans and in the skies, women were put to work, many for the first time, building the weapons of war that were used to defeat the Axis powers. By the time the war ended, the United States of America and the world were completely changed and so were their economies. The dawn of a new age had emerged and nowhere more pronounced than in the United States.

After the war, men were being repatriated and found that the country they left had changed in many ways. It wasn't just the country; they themselves were no longer the innocent farm boys, store clerks and shopkeepers who had left home to fight around the globe but were now men who had faced death and seen the world. Many came home no longer content to plow the farms and sit at home; they craved adventure and excitement. Returning fighter pilots took up motorcycling as a way to relive their glory days, and others found the automobile and the open road more to their liking. Many women, not content to go back and be simple housewives after working and making their own incomes, joined their husbands and boyfriends in these road adventures, and the car culture gripped the population and would never let go.

As the 1950s dawned, America had successfully switched from war production back to consumer goods, and automobiles and the car adventures of the late 1940s blossomed into the golden age of road trips. Families camped, visited relatives and headed west, east, south and north to see the oceans and beaches, mountains and deserts or the many National Parks and forests within easy reach because of the now affordable cars and trucks and station wagons being offered. Families were on the move, rock 'n' roll was on the rise and teenage angst was showing itself with cruising local streets and a growing interest in the hot rod. Teens, especially those in rural towns, found that cars could be a great escape and provide them with not only a career but also relief from the boredom that sometimes creeps into young minds, bragging rights and perhaps fame, by building the fastest hot rod in town or the state. As cars were being built, cruised and raced on the streets all across America, racetracks, dragstrips and other racing venues improved from the early days of auto racing. Manufacturers produced cars with bigger engines, which were faster and had greater horsepower for racing but also used for the family car and station wagons. As the new decade approached, even these relatively mundane family cars began showing up as hot rods.

The 1960s saw the rise of what would come to be called the American muscle car. During Prohibition, moonshiners needed fast cars to outrun the police, which spurred the rumrunners to begin modifying their engines to produce more and more horsepower and handling ability. The cars they produced were so fast that they began entering them in races, and these cars began to dominate the circuits. Oldsmobile, seeing an opportunity, came out with the race-inspired Oldsmobile Rocket 88 production car. In the 1950s, other companies began to produce their own race-inspired engines, with Chevrolet releasing its small-block V8 and Chrysler designing its now famous hemispherical combustion chamber engine, known as the Hemi, in 1955. But it wasn't until the 1960s that the Big Three began their competition to build the fastest production car possible. The 1962 Dodge Dart may not have been the first muscle car built in the '60s, but with its thirteen-second quarter mile time, it was the one to beat. Two years later, the Pontiac Tempest GTO would become the benchmark in muscle car history. To this day, the muscle cars of the 1960s have become the most sought-after cars in the world and a bold statement in American car culture.

As the 1970s dawned, American car companies began to cut corners in a cost-saving effort and as a way to compete with Japanese car manufacturers making inroads into America with cheap and—at the time—less than fully reliable autos. When the disastrous gas shortages hit the country, not only was the cost of the car a major issue but gas mileage became of paramount importance as well. The 1980s saw the Big Three automakers put out a series of cheap plastic and pleather cars that were so bad that they almost fell apart as the new owner left the lot, while Japanese automakers were on the

Cars of all ages, makes and models can be seen to this day as you travel along Route 66.

rise with a much better automobile. Americans were buying more foreign cars in this decade than domestic. What hadn't changed was Americans' love of the road.

Today, only one American car manufacturer, Ford, is still American, and they are almost solely based in Mexico; of the other two, Chrysler was sold to the Italian company, Fiat, and 49 percent of General Motors was given to the auto workers union, with the other 51 percent sold to Canada. Both sales were originated by our government. The largest domestic car manufacturer is Toyota, with Honda running a close second. The cars being produced today have found a good mix of quality and gas savings while providing a sense of luxury in even the least expensive models that would have been unheard of in the 1900s. From the inception of the Model T and into the new millennium, the one thing that hasn't changed and, in fact, has grown over the many years, is America's love of the open road. Road trips are here to stay, and one of the most iconic trips is a tour down the Mother Road of Route 66.

# 2

# THE MOTHER ROAD

*Roads were made for journeys, not destinations.*
*—Confucius*

Route 66 was not the first east to west road in the United States, nor was it the longest. Both the Lincoln Highway, which stretched from New York City to San Francisco, and the Dixie Highway, which ran from Miami, Florida, to Chicago, Illinois, came before the Mother Road, and both, in their own way, had an effect on America. Where these two roads depart from the historic nature of Route 66 is not in their construction, length or destinations—rather it is in the sheer impact that Route 66 had on the country and its population. No other road in history ever affected folks and a nation like the Mother Road did America and what it would eventually become. Route 66, although no longer designated a National Highway, still holds the country in its grip and imagination, and the legend of the Mother Road has now extended past the borders of the United Sates, with hundreds from around the world coming to drive the road, see the architecture and visit the many roadside attractions the route has to offer. As my wife, Terri, said, "Back then, it was the newness and novelty of the road and looking forward. Now, it's the novelty and nostalgia of it and looking back."

The United States is a country always migrating, always moving forward. This has been evident from the time just after the War of Independence, when colonists headed west into the Appalachians and as far as the Ohio Valley. From there, we spread out south and farther west until Americans

Stencils painted all along Route 66 let folks know they are still on the Mother Road, regardless of alignment.

reached the wide Pacific Ocean. Foot trails and river barges gave way to pounded stone roadways used for both military and civilian needs, and railroads soon followed. The horse and buggy, once the preferred method of travel, transitioned to the horseless carriage, and then, seemingly overnight, Henry Ford and Ransom Olds changed the American landscape forever with their "modern" automobiles. With more and more folks driving the ever-improving cars, they began to demand improved roadways. New roads began to be constructed, but many people still couldn't afford the newfangled automobiles—until Ford developed the moving assembly line and began producing the Model T. This car was cheap enough that almost everyone could buy one, and America hit the road with abandon.

Over the next years, with Americans driving mostly dirt roads and less than desirable paved thoroughfares, people began to demand the federal government do something to make their driving lives easier. Washington responded with the Federal Road Act of 1916, but this only allowed federal funds to be used for road improvements. When America entered World War I, these improvements were put on hold while we fought the "Hun." The first interstates weren't authorized until well after the war when the Federal Highway Act was signed into law in 1921. This act allowed for twelve odd-numbered routes running from north to south, and ten even-numbered spanning east–west. The plan for the new roads was accepted in November 1925, and Route 60, running from Chicago to Los Angeles, was laid out in 1926.

One would think that numbering roads would be a simple and easy job; this was not to be the case with Route 60. There were several states that objected to the Chicago–California road, with Kentucky raising the biggest objection. Kentucky felt that the plan completely eliminated it from any of the proposed interstates, that one interstate highway should pass through Kentucky and it should be awarded the designation of Route 60. After the complaints, Kentucky received Route 60, and the Chicago–California route was changed to Route 62. After a few more complaints, the final version of the plan changed the original Route 60 to Route 66.

The eastern terminus in Chicago was originally at the intersection of Michigan Avenue and Jackson Boulevard, but a few years later, it was moved a few blocks east to Lake Shore Drive, otherwise known as US Route 41. While driving Route 66 today, one can find the road rather confusing when trying to negotiate all of the different alignments that the Mother Road has gone through over the years. The western end of the route was first located at Broadway and 7th Streets in downtown Los Angeles and later moved to US Route 101 (now Olympic and Lincoln Boulevards) in Santa Monica. California may have the most alignments of any of the states through which Route 66 travels. Route 66 was designed not only to help facilitate trucking goods to various locations around the country but also to help farmers deliver their crops and meats to market and connect outlying smaller towns and cities that were all but isolated without the new road system. Some of the cities that Route 66 traversed were Springfield, Illinois; St. Louis, Springfield and Joplin, Missouri; Tulsa and Oklahoma City, Oklahoma; Amarillo, Texas; Santa Fe (later bypassed) and Albuquerque, New Mexico; Flagstaff, Kingman, Williams and Oatman, Arizona; and on into California. The original route was officially commissioned with a 2,448-mile stretch; once built, however, it fell short of the mileage mark. The state with the least mileage was, and remains, Kansas, with a grand total length of 13 miles, and it is the only state to have never altered the Mother Road in any way.

One of the reasons that Route 66 has been altered is due to the fact that it was originally conceived to help promote commerce. Once automobiles became affordable and traffic grew along the road, the route began to change to help avoid slower traffic. Many large towns and cities began to be bypassed, which was not a significant problem for those cities and towns that

CALIFORNIA'S HAUNTED ROUTE 66

were near the new alignments, as travelers would still come in to eat, sleep and take in the sights, but cities like Santa Fe became so far removed from the route that many travelers stopped coming to town.

By the mid-1930s, Route 66 was already being touted as the "Main Street of America," and promoters began urging folks to not only drive the route but also start businesses along the roadway. Gas stations, repair shops, places for folks to sleep and eat began to appear, and all helped the economies of the towns and cities along the route. Competition grew among these establishments, and to help lure travelers, more and more garish decorations began to appear. Roadside stops opened small zoos, strange museums, statues and statue gardens and all sorts of odd and fun amusements they hoped travelers wanted to see and spend their money on. Route 66 was redefining the word *kitsch*.

When the Great Depression hit, and the world was thrust into poverty, Route 66 gained its true fame. Having been heavily promoted, Route 66 became the main highway for thousands fleeing west. They sought work in California, which had euphemistically been labeled the "Land of Milk and Honey" by desperate folks looking for salvation. Most of those who arrived in California realized that the "California Dream" was just that—a dream— and most of these same migrants to the west used Route 66 to return home, hoping, as all of America did, that the economic hardships would end. It was during this time, in 1939, that John Steinbeck released his seminal work *The Grapes of Wrath*. The book, dealing with the plight of a family driving to California along Route 66, became a classic read, and it was Steinbeck, in this tome, who first called Route 66 the Mother Road. It would take a world war to end the Depression.

When World War II ended and America repatriated its soldiers, families once again hit the road, and Route 66 was perhaps the most traveled route in America. The small towns along the highway with service stations, eateries and inns survived the Depression due to the migration of the poverty-stricken to California. Those traveling still needed gas, repairs and food, so now that the war was won and America was on the move, these communities began to flourish once again. Unfortunately, this was not to last, and it would be progress that would doom the Mother Road. Dwight D. Eisenhower, supreme commander of the European theater of war, was so impressed by Germany's Autobahn and its ability to transport goods and materiel quickly around the country, realized that if the United States was to remain strong economically and militarily, America needed to develop its own Autobahn-type system. In 1956, President Eisenhower

Since Route 66 followed the rail lines, the railroads are still a big part of Mother Road lore. You will find testaments to this all along the way.

signed the Federal-Aid Highway Act, authorizing five new highways, or interstates, to be built. One of these interstates was I-40, which ran east–west and from Oklahoma paralleled Route 66.

As more and more miles of I-40 were built, the Mother Road slowly began to be bypassed, towns began to decay and Route 66 was mostly left to wear away in the sun, snow and rain, with little in the way of maintenance. Even though a television show, *Route 66*, and a hit song written by Bobby Troup and performed by Nat King Cole "(Get Your Kicks on) Route 66," made the Mother Road a popular "nostalgia" drive, not enough folks were traveling along the route to keep it from dying. By 1985, Route 66 had been officially decommissioned, and that seemed to be the end of an era in car culture and road trips across America; fortunately, this was not to be the case. The Mother Road hadn't died but, for a time, languished in a coma.

Once the road had fallen by the wayside, the public began to realize just what they had lost—not just the history, but the nostalgia, the charm and the romance of a route that had captured the imagination of the country and the innocence that they believed it represented. As the outcry over the loss of the Mother Road grew, the world began to take notice. People from around the globe came to drive Route 66, and its fame grew with each

Motels and motor courts would spring up along the Mother Road where travelers could rest their weary bones. Many are still open today.

traveler. Route 66 was awakening and arising from its long slumber. Local communities, state organizations and tour groups began organizing Route 66 events, trips, tours and festivals honoring the Mother Road. In 1990, Congress passed the Route 66 Study Act, which recognized the Mother Road had "become a symbol of the American people's heritage of travel and their legacy of seeking a better life."

Today, Route 66 enjoys the protection of the National Parks Service and through the Route 66 Corridor Preservation Program receives federal funds and support. Local individuals, nonprofits, local and state authorities and tribal agencies receive money and technical support for the preservation of the route. In 2008, Route 66 had the dubious honor of being placed on the Watch List of 100 Most Endangered Sites. Even with all of the support and funds coming in, the Mother Road is still slowly slipping away into the abyss. It is hoped that more attention to the route will bring more urgency to the highway's plight. I hope this book helps in keeping this wonderful slice of Americana alive for future generations to come.

# 3

# CALIFORNIA'S ROUTE 66

*The road and the tale have both been long, would you not say so? The trip has been long and the cost has been high…but no great thing was ever attained easily. A long tale, like a tall Tower, must be built a stone at a time.*
—*Stephen King,* The Dark Tower

Route 66 from just over the Arizona border, and into California, runs directly through one of the harshest environments known to man, the Mojave Desert. Today, with modern air-conditioned cars, one can safely and comfortably traverse this hot, barren landscape without much trouble. However, in the past, with open cockpit automobiles, cars with no air-conditioning and a roadway not completely paved the whole way, Route 66 could be not only uncomfortable but also deadly. This was what awaited travelers in the early days of east–west migration and family road trips to California.

The beginning of the Mother Road in California starts in the town of Needles. Named for the distinctive peaks east of the city, Needles is the hottest city in all of the United States. Those fleeing the Dust Bowl during the Depression had already faced many challenges, including the Sitgreaves Pass, just a short distance from the Arizona-California border. This pass is so steep that in the early days of automobiles, cars had to ascend in reverse for the lower gear it provided. Many figured that this would be the last obstacle before the salvation of the Golden State. Once they crossed the Colorado River, they realized just how wrong they had been. With temperatures

Unusual sights awaited travelers along Route 66, and many of these sights allowed travelers to spend the night. The Wigwam Motel chain was perhaps the most popular, like this one in San Bernardino, California.

that can routinely reach 110 degrees Fahrenheit or more, many travelers wondered if they had driven into hell itself.

Built along the railroad lines just like most of Route 66, the Mother Road meanders north–south as it heads west to the Pacific coast. One of the reasons for the railroad and route running hither and yon is due to the fact that the Mojave Desert is unlike the stereotypical flat landscape many people think of when a desert comes to mind. California is essentially a mountainous desert region with peaks and valleys scattered all over the southern desert sections. The Cadiz Summit, near the now defunct town of Chambliss, California, with an elevation of 1,302 feet, and the Cajon Pass, with a height of 3,777, were just a couple of the obstacles that awaited travelers in their early automobiles. These mountains and mesas were formed by the San Andreas Fault. Many folks have heard about this destructive force of nature, with movies and television shows making it famous, but the same earthquakes caused by this fault have also made California one of the most beautiful and diverse states in the way of its landscapes than any other in the nation, and Route 66 often runs right along this source of daily quakes.

As difficult as the Mother Road was to drive in the early days, trying to construct a highway in the conditions of the Mojave Desert was worse. It took a stout individual to work in the brutal heat of the day and sometimes into the biting cold of the night. Many a worker suffered from heat exhaustion, dehydration and disease caused by the sudden extremes of the temperature changes, and more than a few perished. As miserable as the work was in these conditions, it was still work—something not easily found in the days of the Great Depression. One of these stalwarts was a man named Walter Knott. Knott would go on to own his own berry farm and help create the delicious boysenberry we all enjoy today.

As Route 66 followed the railroad tracks, many of the stops associated with the rails began to grow along with the traffic. These stops built across the Mojave Desert, such as Amboy, Bristol, Cadiz and so on, were named alphabetically, and many built gas stations, diners, motels and other automobile service–related businesses. As with other Route 66 states, these businesses erected sometimes gaudy signs and unique architecture to lure patrons to their shops, and some of these are still there to this day, albeit few. These stops greatly aided travelers as they made their way across eastern California and beyond. Still, the trek between these stops was grueling.

Past desert oases, silver and borax mining towns, railroad stops, ore processing plants and lots of barren landscapes, travelers kept their eyes on the prize and headed for the promise of a better life in Los Angeles. Once travelers reached, then descended the Cajon Summit and began heading into western San Bernardino County (San Bernardino is the largest county in the United States and stretches from the Arizona border to the Los Angeles County Line. It is 20,105 square miles in area), they began to see a rapid decline in heat and extreme weather patterns. Farther west, farm fields gave way to towns, towns became cities and the cities turned into the metropolis of Los Angeles and Hollywood. Finally, passing through the concrete jungle of downtown and the glamour of Hollywood, the weary traveler reached the sunny shore of the Pacific Ocean.

As happened with most all of Route 66, once the interstates were built, the Mother Road slowly died. This was never more pronounced than in the sweltering heat of the Mojave Desert. The small stops and towns along the winding route saw almost no traffic once Highway 40 opened. Now, able to drive a much straighter and faster route, no one was willing to brave the extreme heat any longer than was needed. Almost all of the towns along the Mother Road have now disappeared. A few, such as Goffs, Amboy and Ludlow, just barely managed to survive, but most have all but vanished from memory. Shortly after Route 66 was decommissioned in 1985, Angel Delgadillo formed the Arizona Historic Route 66 Association (Delgadillo's

*Above*: Even the service stations along the Mother Road were designed to catch the eye of travelers driving down the route.

*Left*: California was not immune to the kitsch that enlivened Route 66, as this giant orange drink stand shows.

Snow Cap Drive-in is still serving food, ice cream and fun in Seligman, Arizona, and is a must-see when driving the Mother Road), and California was soon to follow. In 1990, the California Historic Route 66 Association was established with the sole purpose of preserving Route 66 and keeping the Mother Road's history through California alive for future generations.

Almost all of the original route in California remains, and even though it doesn't have the longest drivable stretch of road (that is reserved for Arizona), it does have the most miles of Route 66 still drivable in the nation. Unfortunately, the stretch of Route 66 between Goffs and Ludlow saw a massive storm and flooding a few years back that washed out many bridges along the road. The State of California is in the process of repairing and rebuilding them, but at the time of this writing, there are still whole stretches of the Mother Road and a few historic towns that cannot be reached. Regardless of when the state finishes repairs, the road from Needles to approximately the town of Rialto is mostly a straight shot; afterward, the route begins to change alignments, and once in the city of Pasadena, the different routes one can take become positively confusing. There are many books out there that will help navigate this jumble of alignments, but some eliminate the shorter ones, ignore others and get a few wrong. For those looking for a comprehensive and accurate map, contact the California Historic Route 66 Association, and its current president, Scott Piotrowski, they won't steer you wrong.

Many people have a view of the route's end tainted by the movie *The Gumball Rally*. At the end of the film, the cars are shown driving onto the Santa Monica Pier as the Mother Road's end. Officially, this is not the case. As confusing as the alignments are running through the city of Los Angles, the route's end can also be just as confusing. There is but one official end to the western terminus of Route 66, and that belongs to the intersection of Lincoln and Olympic Boulevards just a few blocks away from the ocean. There are two other known "ends," and although neither is actually the end of the line, they are, for all intents and purposes, still proper ends for travelers today.

Federal highway rules state that one highway must feed into another; in other words, the highway couldn't end at a dead end. Therefore, the Santa Monica Pier, being a dead end at the Pacific Ocean, could not be used as the terminus. This doesn't stop people from assuming, due to the movie, and that many travelers find their way to the pier once their long drive is finished, that the Santa Monica Pier is in fact the end of Route 66. Even though this is not the case, the Santa Monica Pier has become the "symbolic" end of the

*Above*: Many iconic Route 66 locations have been filmed; some, like the Bagdad Café, shown here, have become famous worldwide.

*Left*: Roy's Motel in Amboy, California, has one of the most recognizable signs along the Mother Road.

route. To commemorate the eighty-third birthday of the Mother Road and to coincide with the opening of his 66-to-Cali store opening on the pier, a past president of the California Route 66 Association placed a trademarked sign on the pier that reads, "End of the Trail." Today, this has become one of the most photographed signs along the route and symbolizes the completion of one's journey along the highway.

The third location stands at the end of Santa Monica Boulevard, where the road meets the Pacific Ocean. In 1952, a plaque was dedicated to the "Will Rogers Highway" as the "spiritual end" of the Mother Road. Many travelers found their end here, high on a bluff overlooking the Pacific, and seeing the pier, they made their way to it and there dipped their feet into the ocean for the first time, their travels finally at an end. Whichever terminus one chooses, or even all three, the traveler will feel a sense of history, accomplishment and joy at having been able to travel the most famous road in American history.

# 4

# GOFFS

*Once a year, go someplace you've never been before.*
*—Dalai Lama*

The tiny, now all but abandoned town of Goffs, California, began as a rail stop. It was known as the town of Blake, in honor of Isaac Blake, builder of the Nevada Southern Railway, which began in the town for points north, between 1893 and 1902. After Santa Fe Railroad took over the failed line, the town was renamed to coincide with the other towns along the tracks, which were named in alphabetical order; it became Goffs. In 1915, Goffs was described as "an old settlement supported mainly by gold, silver and copper mines in the mountains." But its future, and decline, would not come from these metals but from a strip of asphalt.

Goffs began to prosper in the early 1900s as the tent businesses that had sprung up around the railroad moved into permanent structures. With the rail lines keeping folks busy, forty-two of the fifty-eight people living in Goffs in 1910 were railroad employees, and with the many mining ventures flourishing, Goffs was growing. During World War I, the ore coming from the surrounding mines was sought after for the war effort, and this boosted the town's economy greatly.

When the National Old Trails Highway (NOT) was built from Barstow to Needles, it went right through Goffs. By 1916, an average of 40 cars were passing through town daily, and then as most of Route 66 did, the Mother Road followed the rail lines and NOT, so Goffs became a stop for travelers

The Goffs Cemetery is close to the railroad, where phantom trains come whistling past stunned onlookers.

coming into California along Route 66. By 1930, the number of vehicles coming through Goffs had risen to 6,742 a day. Goffs flourished with the influx of travelers, and with so many coming to Goffs, the town grew quickly. In 1914, the town had a post office, school, fuel station, lodgings and everything needed for Route 66 travelers at the time. However, as we have seen, things aren't always certain where Route 66 is concerned. Goffs was only part of Route 66 from 1926 to 1931, and after that year, the town would become mostly a memory of the past.

Goffs's future, like that of many other towns, was dependent on the Mother Road for survival. Route 66 passed directly through the town, but when planners decided to realign the road for a more direct route from Needles to Amboy, Route 66 was moved farther south and well away from the small town. One of the reasons for this new alignment was purely financial. By building this new alignment through the mountains, rather than around them, the California Highway Department could save $245,000 by shortening the route by six miles. This realignment isolated Goffs and put it so far off the Mother Road that traffic all but stopped coming to town. The railroads kept the town alive, albeit barely, but as the folks stopped coming to town and the mines slowed down, the townsfolk began to leave and Goffs slowly died.

The tiny Goffs Cemetery has few graves, and many of those are unmarked. Folks still living here are kind enough to tend to the forgotten.

For a brief time in the early 1930s, Goffs became an air navigation site, but as this was an unmanned, emergency landing strip, it didn't add anything to the sinking economy. By 1937, with so many children leaving with their families, the schoolhouse had shut down, and the remaining children were sent to the town of Essex for their education. By the 1940s, Goffs's population had declined considerably, and even though the army set up a desert training center near the town and used the old schoolhouse as a canteen for soldiers on their way to European battlefields, it still wasn't enough to save the town.

Today, there are approximately fourteen to forty-five folks still living in town. Very few original buildings still remain, and the once iconic grocery store, which also doubled as a dance hall and restaurant, burned down a few years ago. The once dilapidated schoolhouse has been meticulously restored and now functions as a museum for those traveling along Route 66, and it is highly recommended that folks stop to have a look-see. Other items on the museum grounds harken back to a time when Goffs was alive and well,

The town of Goffs may be almost completely gone, but the small museum helps keep it alive with historic structures and equipment on display.

and there is a remote cemetery on museum grounds that holds a few past residents that have decided not leave town, even in death.

The Goffs Cemetery is a short walk from the schoolhouse along a well-maintained dirt path. There are not many folks buried here, but reports from some who have visited the gravesite have claimed to see shadows among the grave markers that disappear as they get nearer the fence surrounding the site. Others have said that while they are paying their respects to those buried here, they have heard whispers, seemingly coming from the air surrounding them, and some have claimed that they have heard their names being called by voices that sound far away.

Another strange event has to do with the railroad that runs directly alongside the cemetery. Folks walking away from the small graveyard have reported hearing the sound of a train coming down the tracks, but when they turn to look, nothing can be seen. Yet the Doppler effect will occur—as if the horn is passing by—and then slowly fades as the phantom locomotive speeds on into the distance.

Goffs may now be nothing more than a memory, but what remains at this town is well worth the stop when driving down this alignment of the Mother Road. Stop in and visit the Schoolhouse Museum, stretch your legs as you view the artifacts laid out in the museum yard and for the intrepid ParaTravelers stopping here, take a stroll out to the cemetery to pay your respects. Keep your eyes open for those that remain; give a listen for those calling to you and you might hear the tell-tale moan of the train whistle.

# 5
# AMBOY

*Oh, the Places You'll Go*
*—Dr. Seuss*

The tiny town of Amboy, California, was established in 1883 as a railroad stop for the Atlantic and Pacific Railroad. The company decided to name all of its depots in alphabetical order, and so, with this stop being the first in the series, it was given the name Amboy. Some of the other stations along the route were Bagdad, Chambliss, Danby, Edson, Fenner, Goffs and so on. Many of these stations are now gone; others have survived, albeit barely, and can still be seen when driving down the Mother Road.

Amboy fared well during its days as a rail stop but never really grew beyond that. There were a few buildings and a place for those on the train to bed down overnight, but not much else. It wasn't until the federal highway system began building what would become a series of intercontinental roads that Amboy blossomed. These roads tended to follow the rails, and the National Trails Highway, precursor to Route 66, went right through Amboy. From the moment Route 66 was built in town, Amboy began to grow. Roughly the halfway point between the towns of Needles and Barstow, Amboy was the obvious place to stop for food and a good night's sleep before trekking on through the Mojave Desert. During the Depression years, Amboy saw an increase in visitors, and even though most didn't have enough money to rent any type of room, they would make camp along Route 66 and purchase

Roy's Motel sign may be the most iconic along the Mother Road.

whatever provisions they could afford before moving on to the coast. The small town was coming into its own.

It wasn't until the end of World War II that Amboy saw its boom days. With the massive surge in tourism and the growing car culture, Amboy saw an influx of tourists that a few years earlier could have only been imagined. The service stations, motels, shops and restaurants began staying open around the clock. As the town of Amboy grew, so did the population. With the township growing, a church and school were built. Then, when a post office finally opened, Amboy residents knew that they were on their way, and nothing could stop Amboy from becoming a proper city. Unfortunately, as we have seen with so many other Route 66 burgs, fate had a different plan for the town in the desert.

When Interstate 40 was built, engineers thought nothing about the towns they were bypassing. It didn't matter to them that they might be destroying these towns, their people and the lives of those who needed the town for their very survival. It wasn't that they didn't care, it was that Washington demanded the straightest, fastest and easiest way to get from point A to point B, and the rail lines were not that. When the new superhighway was complete, Amboy saw an almost overnight decline in traffic, and with that decrease came a drop in income and revenue. It didn't take long for the town to deteriorate, and the folks who once called Amboy home left for greener pastures. By 1976, Amboy was almost completely deserted, and the Mojave Desert began to reclaim the town as its own.

In 1924, Roy Crowl decided to settle in Amboy. It wasn't due to want, but because of circumstances: his car had broken down on the way to Los Angeles, and he didn't have the means to have it repaired, so he and his wife were forced to stay. By 1938, the Crowls had purchased land in Amboy, and Roy opened his own gas station, which he called Roy's Garage. He soon added a café next to the garage and renamed his place Roy's Garage and Café. Not long after, Roy built a few cabins and opened a motel where folks driving the Mother Road could rest for the night in their own semiprivate rooms. He named his new venture Roy's Motel and Cafe. Then, after World War II, Crowl and Herman "Buster" Burris, who owned the town, decided that with the large influx of travelers, turning the motel and attached service station into a twenty-four-hour rest stop would be great for business. At its peak, Amboy had a population of just over seven hundred. When Roy's Motel and Service Station opened, Roy and Herman employed a full 10 percent of those living in town. In 1959, the now famous neon sign that has come to symbolize Route 66 for so many was first erected, just in time for

Although the motel is now closed to overnight visitors, strange things are still seen and heard inside the small rooms and cabins of Roy's Motel.

41

Roy to retire. Many travelers passing through Amboy, both heading to the coast and then returning from their road trip vacations, would talk about Amboy and Roy's Motel, telling others about this "sanctuary from the desert heat." Even with these glowing testimonials, Roy's still couldn't survive the encroaching modernization of America's roadways.

After the town's demise, it went through a series of sales, but it wasn't until 2005, when entrepreneur and businessman Albert Okura stepped in to buy the town and surrounding land, that the long, slow process of trying to bring the town back to life began. By 2008, Okura had managed to reopen the coffee shop, now a small store, and gas station. On November 16, 2019, in front of a large gathering of enthusiasts and after a complete refurbishment, the famous Roy's neon sign was once again switched on.

Today, Amboy is coming back from the dead and rising like a phoenix out of the hot desert sands of the Mojave. There is still a long way to go, but Okura seems to be determined for the town to make a resurgence as it did after World War II. Amboy and Roy's Motel and Café await those driving along the Mother Road who want to catch a glimpse of a once dying icon of Route 66. For those who stop, just be aware that there may be more to the town than its kitsch, neon and Googie architecture. Many believe that the town is haunted, and cults and other nefarious characters may have claimed the town as their own.

There have been numerous stories that have come from the area in and around the town of Amboy. Many believe that satanic cults and demon worshipers have set up shop, hidden somewhere out in the desert looking for victims to use in their evil rituals. There is a story that supposedly comes from a U.S. Marine, who said that while driving from the Marine Corps base in Twentynine Palms to Las Vegas, he was driving the back roads headed for I-40. As he was heading up Kelbaker Road near the town of Amboy, he came across a red car across the roadway completely blocking both directions of the two-lane road. He went on to say that there were a man and a woman lying face-down in the street as if they had been injured or killed. The storyteller related that as a Marine, he was trained to survey a situation and determine the proper course of action from what he saw. To the Marine, something didn't sit right with the scene in front of him, and as he reached for his sidearm, he surveyed the area for a way around. He then carefully drove around the car and the people and, once past, glanced in his rearview mirror. He went on to say that when he looked, the couple on the ground were getting up and that a full twenty people were standing up from hiding places in the tall grass. Needless to say, as he floored his car, he wondered what would have happened to him if he had stopped to try to help. There have been other stories about similar things happening around Amboy. Whether true or simply good fiction, I will leave it up to my intrepid readers.

Another story that is a bit out there was about a woman and her sister driving from San Francisco to New Mexico to see their father. The storyteller said that they stopped in Amboy to see the famous Roy's and had been wandering around for a time snapping pictures, going into the different cabins that were open and entering the motel lobby "illegally" through a window. After exploring the Googie lobby for a time, the woman's sister went outside to have a cigarette. When the storyteller was finally finished, she went looking for her sister but couldn't find her. According to the teller, she entered the gift shop and spoke to the only other person in town, but he hadn't seen the sister either.

The woman went on to say that she wandered around town for a bit calling out her sister's name, and then she suddenly heard her sister's voice coming from inside the Amboy church. Upon entering the church, the storyteller said that she could see her sister near the altar, her hand over her mouth and blood streaming from between her fingers. As she set out to aid her sister, a woman suddenly called for her to stop, and as the storyteller looked at the unknown woman, she noticed that her eyes were completely black and the stranger had a maniacal look on her face. She said that the woman was ranting about a prophet and how she shouldn't get near her sister and all sorts of demonic ramblings. Worried about her sister, the storyteller continued on, but as she led her bleeding sister out of the church, the crazy lady was harassing them, cursing them and scaring the hell out of them.

The woman finished her tale by saying that her sister has never been the same after this encounter, has lost all joy from her life and has not smiled since leaving Amboy. She also stated that once, after leaving the town, she looked at her sister and saw that her eyes were as black as coal, just like the crazy woman's eyes had been. She did say that this only happened once, but she is scared her sister will become just as deranged as the woman who had assaulted her.

There is one more odd tale about Amboy that comes from the annals of the internet. An amateur photographer said that while snapping pictures of the cabins at Roy's Motel, one of the photos came out looking as if there was blood splattered all over the wall. He hadn't noticed this while taking the picture but said that the blood was such a dark red that it looked like it was fresh. He hoped that what he saw was a leftover from a movie or television

Directly behind Roy's sits the Amboy school. Ghosts are said to still haunt the playground and classrooms of this old place of learning.

shoot or perhaps an artwork; however, others on this blog who live near Amboy said that weird things are always happening in the town and that they were not surprised by his discovery. Again, it is up to my readers to determine the veracity of these odd tales.

One thing that has been reported for many years are the tales of spirits still living and wandering the town. One of the most reported occurrences comes from the old Amboy schoolhouse. Reports about ghosts at the school have been coming out since before it closed down in 1999. A former teacher at the school said that many times while working late she would get the feeling she was being watched. She said the feeling was as if someone was intently following her every move, and the discomfort she felt was almost overwhelming. She said that one night, the feeling became so intense she couldn't finish preparing the next day's lessons and had to immediately leave the school.

There were other times when both teacher and student would turn to see who was coming in the front door, only to watch the door slowly open and close as if someone was entering, yet no one was ever seen. At night in the gym, when students were at basketball practice or playing against one of their rivals, things would rearrange themselves while no one was looking and sometimes when they were. Gym bags would be moved from one locker room to the other even though no one was there to have moved the items, and brooms that were carefully placed where they belonged would be found on the opposite wall, or down the hallway or even, on occasion, in a room clear across the other side of the school.

There is one other thing that happened—and still does to this day—and that is on days when there is no wind, the swings in the schoolyard will suddenly begin to swing as if someone is playing on them. Just as fast as the movement began, the swings would come to a complete stop as if they had never been swinging. As with the swings, many folks say that when looking at the school, which is behind an enclosed fence, the feeling of being watched can be overpowering, and there have been reports of people seeing faces looking back at them and then disappearing before their eyes. Other reports that come from the town, albeit only on rare occasions, are of the apparitions of two Native American rail workers who tragically died in an accident near the town. These two are sometimes seen walking the town together and at other times seen alone.

There is one other strange thing that is a complete mystery involving Amboy; it is not paranormal, we think, and it is anything but ominous. In fact, it is something that is a good omen for Amboy and the surrounding Mojave Desert. It would seem that sometime around 2013, two Chinese Guardians appeared four miles east of the town of Amboy directly along Route 66. The two statues are approximately six feet tall, one Yin (female) the other Yang (male), and traditionally known as Fu Dogs. These statues historically guard Chinese palaces, temples, tombs and other places of great importance and often flank the entrances that they guard. The statues stand a quarter mile apart and are more than one hundred yards off the Mother Road, and no one knows how they got there or why.

The Guardians are magnificent in their art, and each imparts both power and serenity when viewed. Traditionally, the male is always set on the right and the female on the left of the place they are charged with protecting, and it is no different here at their place in the Mojave Desert. The male can be seen holding a ball in its left front paw, symbolizing the area is under his protection, while the female statue guards a lion cub under its right paw, symbolizing nurturing and protection of those living in the area. The beauty of their meaning cannot be denied, and one wonders whether the statues were put there or manifested there as a ward against the weirdness that has befallen Amboy and the surrounding area.

Whether you believe the strange tales told on the internet and or the long-held ghost stories that come from the town of Amboy, one thing is clear:

Occult groups and strange gatherings are said to flourish in the Mojave Desert around the town of Amboy. Could it be the Amboy Crater's energy causing these disturbing manifestations?

this historic town, directly on the Mother Road, is one that the intrepid ParaTraveler should not miss. Go see its iconic neon sign, along with its prototypical Route 66 Googie architecture. This town in the desert is one that not only symbolizes the spirit of old Route 66 but also houses spirits from the past that have remained faithful to their town.

# 6

# LUDLOW

*The traveler sees what he sees. The tourist sees what he has come to see.*
*—G.K. Chesterton*

Ludlow, California, is known as the town that died twice. Today, the old railroad water stop may not actually be dead, but it is clinging precariously on life support. Begun in 1882 as a water stop along the Atlantic and Pacific Railroad, the town was named after railcar repairman William B. Ludlow. The small town began to grow in 1900, when gold was discovered at the nearby Bagdad-Chase mine. The first ore yielded seventeen dollars a ton, production stepped up and the mines, along with Ludlow, began to see folks arriving in droves. With the influx of people coming to town, Ludlow, already known for its lack of natural water, had to have even more shipped in to accommodate not only the railroad but its citizens as well. As the water was shipped in, the ore was shipped out to the mills in Barstow and as far away as Oro Grande. In the early 1900s, Ludlow had a bright future ahead.

As the superintendent of the mines had declared the town of Rochester/ Steadman a "closed camp"—which meant no liquor or women were allowed—the miners would come to Ludlow on Friday and Saturday nights to blow off steam and spend their money on booze and soiled doves. This boosted the income of the town immensely, and a hotel, store, saloon, café and pool hall, along with a "boarding" house, soon sprang up in town to cater to the miners. Then, when borax was discovered in the area, a new

*Above*: The town of Ludlow, California, along the Mother Road, is being reclaimed by the cruel Mojave Desert.

*Left*: The Ludlow Café is a must-stop location for good food, milkshakes and to learn about this "town that died twice."

railroad was built that stretched from Ludlow to Beatty, Nevada. Now having three railroads coming to town—the Ludlow-Southern, Santa Fe (once the Atlantic and Pacific) and now the Tonopah and Tidewater (T&T)—Ludlow emerged into a boom time. The citizens figured that as long as the gold, borax and other ores were coming from the mines, the town would not only survive but also prosper.

Unfortunately, in 1916 the Ludlow-Southern Railroad ceased operations, and by 1927, the Pacific Coast Borax Company had begun to move into Nevada. The T&T began to slow and finally shut down in 1933. Even though the Bagdad-Chase mine was still going strong—it is estimated that this mine produced half of all gold mined in San Bernardino County—Ludlow began to decline. As the railroad employees were transferred to other locations and folks began to move out to seek work elsewhere, Ludlow slowly died. By 1925, the population had declined to only a handful, and the community became a ghost town. This was Ludlow's first brush with death.

When the National Old Trails Highway was proposed, the folks still living in Ludlow hoped that it would come through their dead town, and when it was announced that the highway was planned to go straight through, the desert rang with the cheer that came from the few people still hanging on in the town. Then, when Route 66 was established and the traffic increased exponentially, Ludlow saw a renaissance with travelers coming to town for food, fuel and a place for a good night's sleep before heading on to the coast or wherever they were headed in California. The Ludlow Café opened up to serve the hungry; a hotel and then a motel were added to the town; and a service station, store, as well as other places a weary traveler might need, sprang up to provide for them. Ludlow was again booming. Again, this was to be short-lived, and when Interstate 40 was completed and bypassed Ludlow, the town began to decline even faster than it had when the railroads left town.

Ludlow still has folks living there, and a new Ludlow Café has replaced the old one, which had to eventually be torn down due to earthquakes and neglect, and the town survives, albeit barely. The reason for this has to do with its proximity to the interstate. Even though Ludlow was technically bypassed, the town is only a couple blocks off the thoroughfare, and being between Amboy and Barstow, it makes a convenient fuel stop and place to grab some grub. The town still has a motel in which one can stay, but you have to head to the gas station for info and to check in. As stated, the town is still alive yet on life support. It may be because the town is still living that quite a few dead townsfolk are still in Ludlow, or it could just be they can't stand to see their town falling apart. Whatever the reason, Ludlow is well known for its wandering spirits both in the cemetery and the town itself.

The Ludlow Cemetery is not hard to find, but it is not exactly easy to get to. You have to drive down Ludlow Road to the west, cross the railroad tracks and then drive back east to Bagdad-Chase Road to look for the cemetery. Or you can simply drive down Main Street, park when you catch a glimpse of the place and cross the tracks on foot; then it's a short walk to the cemetery. Whatever way you decide to go, the ParaTraveler may be in for more than they bargained for. It is said that both day and night, folks can see the spirits of the dead walking among the wooden crosses. Many speculate that the reason so many specters move among the markers may have to do with the fact that most of the crosses are now falling over or that many have no names attached to them. It is well known that the dead do not like being buried, nameless and alone, so this theory may be a good one to keep in mind while walking in the graveyard.

It is said that at night, folks who are in or near the cemetery can hear the sounds of conversations that have no source and seem to be simply carried on the wind. Paranormal investigators and ghost hunters alike have heard the dead asking why they are dead, but even if the living respond, no further inquiries are heard in response. It is believed by some that the spirits are not asking the living why they are there but talking to the other ghosts they are with. For those who venture into the cemetery, especially in the evening hours, try not to be afraid, but remember that you may be surrounded by the spirits of people, just like you, only incorporeal.

The town of Ludlow also has a few spirits that like to make themselves known. The old Pendergast Hotel, now abandoned and decaying in the harsh desert sun, seems to have at least one ghost that will let people know it is there by banging on the walls inside the crumbling structure and sometimes calling out to those nearby. During the daylight hours, folks have reported seeing shadows walking around in the empty building, and at night, a strange light moves about. No one knows who the specter might be, but the spirit seems to be very active.

Another spirit in Ludlow can be seen simply strolling along the streets— although seen on different roads within the town, the ghost, as described by those who have seen him, is always the same. Folks have said that he is dressed as an early rail worker would have been and is most likely one of the many folks killed by the speeding trains that passed through the town. Other folks have said that while passing through Ludlow itself, they can see garage doors, storage sheds and other egresses open and close of their own accord.

The Ludlow Cemetery, like so many others along Route 66 in the Mojave Desert, is crumbling and a place where unmarked graves fade into time and out of our memories.

Ludlow, like many other towns along the Mother Road in California, is one that any ParaTraveler should make a point to visit. The café just outside of the town has good food, and the owners and employees are a wealth of historical info on the town. The motel, while rustic, allows you to be right in the heart of the paranormal activity for those looking for such. Even if you aren't staying in town, it is highly recommended to stop in, have some lunch, dinner or a milkshake and see this historic piece of Route 66 for yourself.

# 7

# CALICO GHOST TOWN

*Travel is not reward for working, it's education for living.*
*— Anthony Bourdain*

Only about three miles off National Trails Highway, Route 66, stands one of the most complete, albeit rebuilt, ghost towns in California. Now a tourist stop for those coming or going to Las Vegas, Calico Ghost Town was not only one of the most productive silver mining camps in the state but also one of the most historic. Because of this, the State of California has designated Calico as the official Silver Rush Ghost Town of California. From its humble beginnings to its being the inspiration for a Southern California amusement park, Calico Ghost Town has become a fixture within the Mojave Desert and a place for families to learn about mining, life in the harsh desert and a place where fun can be had for all. It is also a must-stop for every ParaTraveler who craves the enjoyment of visiting with spirits, and Calico has many.

Calico had its beginnings when four men were looking for a red vein of ore found years earlier by one of the men's fathers in the Calico Mountains. It is said that the name of the mountains came from the multicolored rocks that dominate the landscape. Needing a grubstake, the men approached San Bernardino Sheriff John King, who agreed to fund the claim, and the Silver King Mine, named in honor of the sheriff, was formed. The mine was so successful that word spread, and those seeking their fortune began showing up and staking claims all over the area. Soon, corporations from the east

Miners would build their homes out of discarded wood, boxes and even the hillsides themselves.

began to buy up these claims and open new ones, and the population grew to the point that a town was inevitable.

The location of Calico was dictated by those who had already set up lean-tos and makeshift shelters on the only semi-level area close to the main mining claims and just below King Mountain. Surveyed in the summer of 1882, by October of the same year, a road had been built and construction begun on the town of Calico. The name is most likely derived from the mountains that bear the same name; however, there is a story that says a miner, watching the town being built, commented that "this town will be as pretty as a gal's calico skirt." Whichever is true, the name of the town became Calico.

As the town grew, the number of those coming in to find their fortune grew even faster. Whenever a new claim was filed, lean-tos, shacks made out of old crates and canvas or holes dug into the ground itself would be found as close as possible to the miners' claims. Even the hills were hollowed out and caves dug for miners to live in, and today, one can visit Calico and see "homes" built with nothing more than fallen rocks and stones under overhangs and hollows in cliff faces. Anywhere a miner could find to live, they did. These makeshift abodes were not restricted to living quarters; public venues also used the natural surroundings to their benefit. One "hotel" that billed itself as the "finest lodging in Calico" was the Hyena House Hotel. When patrons of the hotel arrived in town, they would see a sign reading "Free bus to the Hyena"; a coach (a wheelbarrow) was waiting by the sign to take them to their lodging. When they arrived at Hyena House, they found the hotel was nothing more than holes dug into the rock outcropping, covered with burlap sacks for privacy and supported by old barrels. In the desert, nothing was discarded and all was repurposed.

Life in the Mojave Desert was never easy, but living high above the desert floor made things even more difficult. Water, the most important thing for survival, had to be shipped in, rationed and paid for; foodstuffs needed to be preserved; and "desert coolers" constructed for this purpose, along with everything else that made life bearable, had to come from miles away, up the sloped street and delivered daily. Life at Calico was always a challenge. It took a hearty, hardy soul to survive, and those were found in abundance at this town in the desert. One such pioneer was Lucy Lane.

Lucy came to Calico as a young girl in 1884, spent most of her childhood here and only left once as a child to attend school for two years in the town of Spadra, California. As Lucy grew, she and her siblings would pick through the tailings, the leftover dust and debris from a mine, and collect bits and pieces of ore to supplement their allowances. With what they collected, they would order clothes and other things they wanted from a Sacramento store catalogue. In this way, Lucy learned the value of hard-earned money and the ways of mining. When she married John Lane, a man many years older, she also learned good business practices while helping her neighbors at the same time. Lucy and John became friends with most of the townsfolk. If a neighbor needed credit, the Lanes extended it; if a neighbor needed help, the Lanes were there to lend a hand. Community was more important to the Lanes than wealth, and because of this, the Lanes would become key figures in the town of Calico.

As the silver market began to diminish, so did Calico. Folks looking to the future realized that many of the mines were played out, and those that were still producing could barely provide enough cash to survive. Many moved out of town to seek their fortunes elsewhere. By the 1940s, Calico was all but abandoned, with Lucy being the only resident remaining after John passed away. Lucy Lane would go on to live at Calico for eighty-three years, passing away in 1967. During her time, Lucy had seen the town thrive, almost burn to the ground and come close to fading away and then watched as a rebirth took place with her as a centerpiece and ambassador of its growing popularity. Lucy is buried next to her husband in San Jacinto Cemetery in

Calico was all but gone when Walter Knott bought the town to restore it to its former glory. *Courtesy of the Mojave River Valley Museum.*

the town of San Jacinto, California. It is said that Lucy has never left her beloved Calico, and even to this day she looks after the town that was her home for so many years. The town suffered several devastating fires that had reduced Calico to a mere handful of buildings, and those, other than the one Lucy lived in, were being reclaimed by the desert. It looked as though the town of Calico would be lost like so many other mining camps, fading away into nothing more than a memory. But then Walter Knott stepped in and saved the town that he had grown to love so many years earlier.

Walter Knott was the nephew of John King, the man who had put up the money that started the claim and gave birth to the desert town. Knott worked as a carpenter in Calico in the early days of the twentieth century but had left the town to help construct the new Route 66 roadway making its way through the desert. During his time at Calico, Knott had grown to love the town and even used it as his inspiration for the roadside attraction that would bring folks to his berry farm. It was at this berry farm where Knott and Rudolf Boysen created the now popular boysenberry. Having used the town as the model for his "Calico Ghost Town" exhibit at what would become Knott's Berry Farm Amusement park in Buena Park, California, Knott simply could not allow the town to fade into history.

John and Lucy Lane. *Courtesy of the Mojave River Valley Museum.*

Walter Knott had made a lot of money off his berry farm after helping create the boysenberry. Along with his tourist ghost town and his wife's thriving chicken restaurant, Knott had made enough money to realize his dream of saving Calico. When Knott bought the town in 1951, there wasn't much left of it: a handful of buildings, a few sheds and some mining equipment. It took quite a few years, and a lot of research, but slowly the old mining town was brought back to life. During the restoration, Knott opened Calico to visitors, allowing them to see the town, its history and his vision for what it would become. Lucy Lane, who still resided in town, became the official greeter and hostess, regaling guests with stories of the past and showing them what life had been like during Calico's heyday and what it was like for her to still be living in the town. The money brought in from visitors all went toward the town's rebirth, and many who came gave much more than was asked. Calico had a bright future, and it was all thanks to the man who had a lifelong connection to the town and who had made his fortune from building its replica far from the town itself.

In November 1966, with the restoration complete, Walter Knott turned over the ownership of Calico, free of charge, to the County of San Bernardino. The only stipulation he placed on the county was that Calico remain as it was, a place for people to come and learn about the early days of mining in California in a fun environment. San Bernardino has so far made good on this commitment. Today, Calico has become a tourist town, with shops, food and tours of one of the original mines. There is even a campground and cabins for rent, allowing guests to stay in the heart of the history that is still on display in the town. Every year, the town hosts events such as Calico Days, which highlights the town's history and importance to California, and a holiday display that showcases how Christmas must have been for the miners. Perhaps the most attended event that Calico hosts is its Halloween haunts event. This event is spread over two weekends at the end of October and celebrates all things ghostly at the town, which makes perfect sense considering there seems to be a spirit in every single building at Calico. Yes, the town may be the most haunted place in the country.

To say that Calico is haunted would be an understatement. When doing research for my book *Ghosts and Legends of Calico*, I wasn't sure how much

Walter Knott and his wife, Cordelia, at the dedication of Walter's monument in Calico Ghost Town. *Courtesy of the Mojave River Valley Museum.*

activity a small, touristy, historic town could possibly have. I would soon find out that just about every place in the town, including the Maggie Mine, had reports of paranormal activity. I was once told by the rangers who oversee Calico that "we are a historic ghost town, not a historic town of ghosts." One wonders if they know the true extent of Calico's past residents that still call the town home.

There are a few places within Calico that serve food and snacks; there is even a shop that caters to the needs and appetites of our canine friends. Each of these shops and eateries is unique in what it serves, but they all have one thing in common: each has its own ghost. Lil's Saloon began life as the doctor's office and pharmacy. Not having much need for either in a tourist stop, the building near the center of town was repurposed to serve pizza, hot dogs and beer. The town provides entertainment in the form of mock shoot-outs, fun rapport between outlaw and sheriff and other amusements. Over the years, the actors would relax in Lil's once the day was through, and it has now become a tradition. There are times, however, when the employees of Lil's will be working in the back, cleaning and closing up after all have left and hear the sound of people carrying on in the dining room. They will go to investigate the sound, figuring that some cast members, not realizing the saloon was closed, are waiting for service. The talking continues right up until they enter the dining room. As soon as they enter the room, all noise stops and the room is completely empty. Other times, guests sitting at their tables feel as if someone has brushed past them even when no one has passed by.

The Old Miners Café, sitting up on a hill near the schoolhouse, seems to have spirits who argue with each other and another that likes to move things around in the stockroom and on occasion toss buns at the cook. The two popcorn carts in town have spirits attached to them as well. Perhaps the most interesting dining experience comes from the only full-service restaurant in town, the Calico House Restaurant. Here you will find a spirit who likes to turn up the radio so loud that one cannot hear themselves think and likes to call out people's names at random times. Perhaps the most disturbing thing that happens at the Calico House comes about when the restaurant is closed. It is not unheard of for a mysterious shadow figure to be seen crossing the street in front of the eatery and passing into the lot on the opposite side. This usually happens after dark, and many taking the nightly ghost walk tour have seen this strange apparition.

The Sweet Shop, near the top of the town, has a little boy spirit that is often seen running up the street, darting into the candy store and ducking

*Above*: One of the few remaining original buildings, Rhea's doctor's office and drugstore has been repurposed as Lil's Saloon.

*Right*: The Sweet Shop has a small boy spirit that not only likes candy but also plays hide and seek with the employees.

into the back room. No one is sure who the child is, but he has been seen so often that everyone who works at Calico know about him. He has become such a figure in town that he was given the name Johnny. The boy has been known to respond to that name. Next door to the Sweet Shop is Dorsey's Dog House. Named after Dorsey, the mail-carrying dog that actually carried the mail at Calico for a time, this store caters to dogs and sells treats, leashes and all things a man's best friend could ask for. It also seems to have an undefined spirit that sometimes takes the form of a post or blends into the surroundings so well that one may think they are just looking at a piece of the building. Who or what this spirit may be is unknown.

The Maggie Mine was one of the working mines at Calico, and as it sits directly in town and is completely safe to enter, it has become a favorite attraction to walk through for those visiting the town. It is also a great place to cool down in the hot Mojave Desert sun. There is a legend that comes from the Cornish miners of old about fairy creatures known as tommyknockers. These kin to Scottish brownies and Irish leprechauns are said to inhabit mines, both helping and hindering the work of their human counterparts— helping if the humans are kind to them and hindering or perhaps killing their counterparts if they are unkind or overly mean. The tommyknockers were widely believed to be real, and many of the local miners believed that tommyknockers inhabited the Maggie Mine. Many folks touring the mines today have reported odd things happening that are less ghostly but still odd, and those at Calico believe that the guests are hearing and sensing the tommyknockers still at work in the mine.

The tommyknockers are not the only strange things going on in the mine. There have been many reports of people hearing voices in areas of the mine that are off-limits and fenced off. The sounds of drilling machines, hammers and picks hitting the stone of the shafts and even snoring coming from a mannequin placed on a cot in the rest area across from the "glory hole" have all been reported. The strangest tales come from the exit area in the back of the mine. Here, a set of steps ascend to the door leading outside. On many occasions, folks have told of seeing what looked like zombies, all dressed as miners, descending the staircase as if on their way to work. Many people have fled in terror at the sight of these undead mine workers, but none of the apparitions has ever deviated from the trek, nor even seemed to notice the living. If you are lucky enough to see this for yourself, keep watching and see where they are headed.

There are many shops at Calico, all selling different things a tourist might crave. There is the leather shop, selling all things hide derived, including

This stairway leading to the exit of the Maggie Mine is where folks have seen "zombie-like" spirits seemingly on their way to work in the mine.

some excellent gun belts. There is a candle store, a rock shop and an art museum, a kid's toy store and a general store, as well as a place to buy books on the Old West and the town itself. All of these places sell different items, and all are haunted. An employee in the store that was once the undertaker's parlor told me that "just because things move on their own inside the shop, it doesn't mean it's haunted." I just smiled and agreed with her.

One of the places that seems to have the most activity would be R&D Fossils and Minerals. This store sells everything from gems and stones to magnets and clothes. It also may be the home of the town's founder, Sheriff John King. King has been seen walking in the store, following shoppers, and seems to hate Elvis Presley music. Every time Elvis is played, the radio will suddenly turn off or the dial will be switched to country music. King has also become protective of those who work at the store. He will sometimes be seen sitting in the office chair, watching the store as if keeping an eye on things. The manager's son, who had never been in the store before, was helping out one day, made a joking aggressive comment toward his mother, and they both heard the sound of heavy boots heading toward her son. The manager

Calico is a great place to spend the day while traveling along Route 66.

called out, "John, he's my son and is joking." As soon as she spoke out, the boot treads stopped, and they heard them retreat back to the office door.

Other shops that have a fair amount of activity are the candle shop, a woodworking store and the Calico Print Shop. The Print Shop sells books and other tourist fare and seems to have a cowboy that can be a bit mischievous but also seems to like kids. The Lane General Store is the same building where Lucy and John Lane had their store, and it would seem that both of the Lanes are still there keeping an eye on the clerks and the customers. John has been seen from time to time, and his cigar smoke is often present during working hours. Lucy has been seen so often walking to or from the store to the Lane House directly across the street that it is no longer even questioned whether her spirit is still at Calico.

From longtime beloved street performer "Tumbleweed" Harris and the Calico town "sheriff" to Dorsey the dog on the porch at the Calico Print Shop, along with the old schoolmarm who still teaches her students at the schoolhouse, there is little doubt that Calico has its fair share of ghosts still calling the town home. The cemetery, with its lost graves, mines that echo the voices of those lost to accidents and even the town office—where I was told ghosts don't exist—having many tales of the soiled doves who called the building home appearing to visitors, Calico certainly put the ghosts into the term *ghost town*.

# 8

# THE HARVEY HOUSE

*Map out your future—but do it in pencil.*
*The road ahead is as long as you make it. Make it worth the trip.*
*—Jon Bon Jovi*

When Route 66 was first planned, it was laid out along America's rail lines. The reason for this was that before the tracks were placed, an extensive survey was done to find the flattest, easiest and most direct route possible following those guidelines. If one is constructing a road for travelers, especially when taking into account the new, not well powered and still somewhat experimental automobiles of the time, it made sense to follow the route already there and mapped. Another advantage of placing the Mother Road along the railroads was that many lines, most notably for Route 66 the Atchison, Topeka and Santa Fe (AT&SF), already had tourist shops, hotels and restaurants that could be used by those taking part in the burgeoning road trip culture beginning in America. For the AT&SF, this meant stopping at one of the now famous Harvey House Hotels and Restaurants that were spread every one hundred miles along the lines; travelers along the Mother Road could and would use these same stops. Many of these Harvey House Hotels are still standing to this day, albeit with other uses than their original design.

Fred Harvey immigrated to the United States from London when he was just fifteen years old. When he arrived in New York City in 1850, he took a job in a restaurant, and this began his long career in the food service

The Casa del Desierto is one of the few remaining Harvey Houses in California.

industry. Moving around from city to city and restaurant to restaurant, Fred studied both the business and food aspects of being a restaurateur from New York to New Orleans. He finally landed in St. Louis, where he worked until he was ready to open his own fine-dining establishment. Unfortunately, this endeavor failed. Having worked as a mobile mail clerk in the booming railroad business during the American Civil War, after his restaurant went belly-up, Harvey once again took a job with a railroad, the Atchison, Topeka & Santa Fe. This time, however, it wasn't dealing with mail but with the line's food service. At that time, food was not served onboard the trains, and if a passenger wanted food, they had to wait until the train came to a station or rest stop, jump off the train and either eat at the railroad's small food shop or head into town. If a passenger was late getting back from the town, it usually meant the train would leave without them; if they ate at the stop, it generally meant they would be served a meal that was barely palatable. Harvey saw a need for better food and service, so he came up with an idea.

Fred Harvey thought that having a place close to the stations and rails that catered solely to the needs of the passengers, not run with the distractions of other rail concerns, would not only be profitable but also good for the AT&SF's reputation. The company president Charles F. Morse agreed and allowed Harvey to open a dining room in the home Santa Fe depot of Topeka, Kansas, as a test case in 1876. Harvey didn't cut corners, and the menu, while featuring steaks, fresh potatoes and vegetables, wine, beer and delectable desserts, was served at a reasonable price in a dining room with imported linens, exemplary service and china that featured the Fred Harvey name. The restaurant was so successful that it wasn't long before Harvey bought a hotel to go along with his eatery. Over time, Harvey opened up more and more hotels and eateries along the Santa Fe rail line, and his venture became the first "chain of restaurants" in the United States. At first, Harvey had an all-male staff; the waiters, while efficient, seemed indifferent to the guests, and as folks began to mention the "uncaring" service, Harvey decided to make a change. Enter the Harvey Girls.

In 1883, Harvey completely changed the waitstaff to all-female waitresses. Before a lady could become a Harvey Girl, she had to be educated and then graduate from Harvey's school. This school taught the women how to be proficient in not only waitressing but also customer service, manners and efficiency. Being a Harvey Girl became such a sought-after position that ladies from around the country flocked to the school in the hopes of being hired. After graduation, the women chose where they wanted to work and were given a first-class train ticket to the location, provided free room and board and given an excellent wage. With their iconic black dresses and bows, perfectly starched white aprons and caps, along with the renowned reputation of good looks, fine manners and superb service, they became immortalized in the 1946 musical *The Harvey Girls*, featuring Judy Garland.

Each Harvey House built along the railroad was designed with the location's local flair in mind. Harvey establishments in New Mexico, for

The Harvey Girls became famous for their superb service, manners and skill.

instance, featured Pueblo-style architecture, and the cafés served local dishes to reflect the tastes of the population of the area. Each was unique, had its own style, and was named in honor of the area where it was established. So popular were the Harvey Houses, even after they closed down, many of those who worked in and visited these establishments have remained, even after death.

The Casa del Desierto, or House of the Desert, in Barstow, California, sits directly on an old, short Route 66 alignment. The road used to meander across the Mojave River, then back again, and went past the Barstow Harvey House before changing alignment for good, which now is today's Main Street. Originally built in 1885 out of wood, the Casa del Desierto became one of the most frequented of the Harvey Houses in California. Unfortunately, the depot, restaurant and hotel burned to the ground in 1908. The depot and Harvey House we see today was constructed between 1910 and 1913 and portrays the regional aesthetic influences in design of Santa Fe sixteenth-century Spanish and Southwest Native American architecture. The Casa del Desierto became Santa Fe's rail "hub" servicing the rail line's other depots within California.

Barstow today is known mainly as a stop to fuel up, get some lunch or dinner and pick up snacks for the road ahead. It is here that Interstate 15 continues on to Las Vegas, Nevada, and where Interstate 40 begins its long journey to points east. One can jump on and off to drive those parts of the Mother Road still drivable through the desert. But when the Harvey House was rebuilt and opened in 1913, Barstow was the Santa Fe passenger rail transfer hub. It was here that those coming in from Chicago and other points east would change trains to continue to their travel destinations of Los Angeles, San Diego and San Francisco. As some connections didn't depart for hours or days after arriving at the depot, the Harvey House was the place to stay and dine while waiting. For those who had connections that were only hours away, the Harvey House offered a place to eat, enjoy entertainment and admire the beautiful desert scenery.

When entering the Casa del Desierto, one was greeted by a posh lobby, where one could check in for the night or chose one of the two dining rooms, the east-end ballroom on the right, which was the formal room, or the west-end dining room, which was meant for a less well-to-do crowd or those who wanted a more relaxed dining experience. The formal dining room required men to wear dinner jackets, or they could borrow one from the rack, to be returned when finished. If one was not formally attired, you could still enter and sit at a table; however, you would not get any service. The west-end room

The Harvey House today has different uses than in the past, but it still functions as an Amtrak Depot.

required no jacket or formalwear and featured a semi-horseshoe-shaped lunch counter that seated fifty people. The one thing that remained the same in each dining room was the quality of the food and service, depending of course on one's attire in the formal dining room.

The height of train travel popularity for the Casa del Desierto was from roughly the 1920s through the 1940s, and it was during this time that a train would stop at the depot every thirty minutes at one of the eight platforms. These platforms are still there today.

During World War II, the Harvey House saw its greatest business. With so many soldiers and military personnel passing through on their way to one of the many government instillations and transport docks along the California coast, the need to house them while they waited for their connecting train was almost overwhelming. But the Harvey Houses sustained the crush and did it with the same attention to detail that they would with any guest. As happened with so many other forms of travel, World War II was not only the era of the greatest business but also spelled the doom for rail travel and the Harvey Houses.

War is always a catalyst for invention and improvement of past inventions—World War II was no different. From the beginning of the global conflict, airplanes and, in particular, jet aircraft, were no exception;

with every combatant country vying for the first operational jet aircraft, the die was cast for the future of aviation. After the war was won, aircraft manufacturers turned to civilian air carriers with their new designs, and once these companies began offering flights that could get passengers to their destinations days earlier than any train could ever imagine, train travel saw a massive decline in ridership. With the decrease in riders, the businesses that catered to these passengers began to suffer to the point that it was no longer feasible to remain open—such was the case with the Harvey Houses.

By the end of the 1950s, the Barstow Harvey House had seen a steady decline in visitors, and it wasn't long before the hotel closed and then the dining rooms. All that remained at the once bustling Santa Fe train depot was a small station lobby that served few passengers and the machine shop to which Santa Fe had leased the rest of the building. Once Amtrak came into existence, it took over the lobby and included a small cafeteria, but by 1974, Santa Fe was already in the works to have the Casa del Desierto demolished to add even more space to its already huge rail yard. Luckily, a group of concerned citizens objected to the destruction of the now famous and historic train depot and managed to collect enough money to have the Casa del Desierto placed on the National Register of Historic Places. In 1976, the Harvey House was designated a California Historical Landmark. Some of the money raised went toward the ongoing restoration of the old depot, and in 1985, Santa Fe, tired of having to deal with the building and ongoing work projects, donated the depot to the City of Barstow. The city officially purchased the property in 1990, and in 1992, Barstow was about to rededicate the Harvey House as complete when the massive Landers earthquake struck. It would take two more years to repair the damage.

Today, the building functions as a municipal office and an Amtrak stop and hosts events in the two restored dining rooms. It also houses both the Western America Railroad Museum and the marvelous Route 66, Mother Road Museum. This museum is a must-see when driving the Mother Road. With the history, the massive amount of people who stayed here and the dreams and aspirations of those passing through, it shouldn't come as a surprise that this wonderful relic of the past would be haunted.

Tales of the supernatural have been coming from the Barstow Harvey House long before the station was closed in the 1960s. One such apparition is a man known as Buchanan. This gentleman is said to be the spirit of a man who was crushed between railcars while working in the railyard out in front of the station. When his would-be rescuers arrived, they knew that the

Once the informal dining room, this area now hosts events.

man was beyond help, so they asked him if he had anything he wanted to say before he succumbed to his injuries. Buchanan's dying wishes were to speak to his beloved wife and family one last time and to have a cigarette once more before he died. He wasn't able to see his family before he passed, but he died with the cigarette between his lips.

It is not hard to tell when Buchanan is nearby, as the smell of cigarette smoke will be very noticeable. As the State of California has banned all smoking indoors, it is not hard to mistake the aroma. As mentioned, tales about Buchanan have been coming from the Casa del Desierto long before it stopped being a rail depot. Folks waiting for their trains would report seeing a gentleman standing by the door and looking out as if waiting for someone to arrive. He would stand there for a minute or two and then simply fade from view as they watched. Could it be that Buchanan was watching for his family so he could say goodbye and finally pass on? It is said that during restoration, this spirit would oftentimes be glimpsed watching those at work and would sometimes be seen trying to assist in the labor. Even today, folks working in the offices of the Harvey House and those staffing the small welcome desk in the lobby will catch the smell of a cigarette just before they see a wispy figure appear nearby. It would seem that Buchanan has yet to find what is keeping him tied to the mortal plane. It is hoped that one day this gentleman spirit will find peace and pass on.

As with the other rooms, the once formal dining room is used for various events and parties.

A blogger by the moniker Dynamic Writer wrote this about the Harvey House in 2013: "A shadow lingered around the corner of my eye as I began to approach the railroad depot. I felt hot wind touch my face. I was later greeted by a cold draft upon entering the front door. [It was] as if someone was running out the front door, spirit-wise." This is a common theme of those entering the Casa del Desierto, which allows paranormal investigators to book private investigations at the Harvey House. According to those who have visited the old depot for this reason, it is rare that they leave without having witnessed some sort of paranormal activity.

Psychic medium and friend Victoria Ruffulo has investigated the Barstow Harvey House a number of times and said this about what she has found at the Casa del Desierto:

*We are always greeted by the Harvey Girls when we arrive, these spirits treat us with utmost respect and hospitality. The staff at the Harvey House is always present and welcoming. There are other spirits here however, who not only want to leave, but are unable to pass on for various reasons. One such spirit is a man down in the basement of the depot. I first met this spirit when a group of us went down the stairs, as I set foot on the dirt floor, I was immediately drawn to an area where I heard a male voice pleading for help. He kept repeating, "Stop, stop, help, please." I began to feel a pain in my head, had a hard time breathing and dropped to the floor. I realized that what I was feeling was the spirit being hit on the head by two other men with shovels. The next thing I felt was dirt being thrown over me as if I was being buried alive. After this, the spirit described himself as a drifter whom the other men despised and had decided to murder. The entire experience was horrific.*

*While these feelings had been washing over me, my husband, Joe, saw that I was distressed, and the tour guide we were with came over and between them convinced me to head outside for fresh air and regain my bearings. As I left the building and headed for the trains next to the Harvey House, I felt the tortured spirit of the drifter leave me. The tour guide's wife was already outside, and as I explained to her what had happened, she told me that the same thing had happened to her. She told me that after her encounter with the spirit in the basement, she had done research and had found that there had been a man buried in the basement exactly where the two of us had our experiences.*

*Joe and I went back to the Casa del Desierto a few years later and went back to the basement to see if the spirit had finally passed on. I found him still there, and this time he told me that all he wanted was to not be forgotten and that he was scared. I told him that no matter what, I would never forget him. He seemed relieved after I told him this, and all feelings of fear and longing that I had felt from him left me.*

*There is a little girl that is well known at the Harvey House, but few know about her playmate and brother. I was told that they are waiting for their father; they say that he is due on the next train. Their mother is there with them, and she always tries to stop them from running out the front doors but is never successful. The mother never seems to notice me or anyone else.*

*The kitchen is always busy, and the walkway to the dining room is filled with staff waiting to serve their guests. I have seen guests waiting in the dining rooms, eager to taste the wonderful food, and have heard their laughter as they enjoy each other's company. All in all, I can honestly say that the Harvey House has its share of spirits, both happy and sad.*

Buchanan is not the only resident spirit haunting the Harvey House. The spirit known as Rachel is often seen walking along the balcony of the Casa del Desierto. No one knows who this fetching woman is, with some claiming she is a former Harvey Girl, still going about her business, while others say she is the bride-to-be of a soldier coming home from war, a man who has yet to return. Because of the differences in the storyline of this walking spirit, there are two tales of her demise. In the case of the first theory, the tale states that as a Harvey Girl, she was nice to a male customer who had gotten the wrong idea about her kindness and approached her in a romantic way, but on being rejected by the young woman, her would-be suitor killed her in a fit of rage. This act has doomed her to an eternity of haunting the place she was murdered—or at least an essence of her was doomed. In the second theory of how this young lady passed, it is said that while waiting for her true love to come back from war (it is assumed by her attire to have been World War I), this young lady realized that her beloved was never coming home and jumped from the balcony to her death. From the reports of those who have seen her, it appears that she is a residual haunting brought about by the extreme emotion of either scenario. For those who do not know what a residual haunt is, picture a video loop that plays over and over without the ability to stop playing. This is in direct contrast to an intelligent haunting where the spirit is conscious and able to interact with its surroundings.

There is another distinct spirit here that has been seen and heard many times since the train depot has been closed, and that is the ghost of a little girl. No one knows who this child is, and no one knows why she stays around at what is now a remote, out-of-the-way bastion of past travel. There are no records of a child passing away at the Barstow Harvey House, nor any records, that can be found anyway, of a child who passed away in transit between the Casa del Desierto and the previous train stop. Regardless of who she may be, she has been known to be a pleasant child who likes to play. This little girl is seen mainly in the lobby of the Harvey House and the adjacent staircase. Folks coming in will suddenly hear the sound of her laughing and giggling, trying to lure the living into a game of tag, and will play a spectral game of peek-a-boo for those willing. For those who have investigated the Barstow Harvey House, many have also found her hiding in one of the old dining rooms and following them from room to room as they investigate. Often, these investigators will hear her let out a giggle and, on reviewing their audio recorders, hear her running around, talking to them and engaging them with playful, spectral commands. There have even been times when folks have caught her shedding a tear when she has been unable to get the living to play with her.

The Harvey Girls were never just employees to Fred Harvey. He treated all of his staff as family. Even in a time when women were still considered second-class citizens in some quarters, Harvey knew women to be as hard working and every bit as conscientious as men. Because of this, he put great faith and responsibility in his waitstaff. The women who came to work at the Harvey Houses, many being treated as equals for the first time in their lives, became devoted not only to their careers but also to the man who treated them so well. With a love for the man and his business, it should come as no surprise that many of the Harvey Girls would come back, after death, to a place where they felt they belonged.

The Barstow Harvey House has been added to the list of historic places.

Reports of seeing Harvey Girls in their distinct black dress and bow, wearing the white apron emblazoned with the Harvey House name, still going about their business in the two dining rooms have been numerous. The girls have been seen moving between the central kitchen and invisible tables, carrying trays, then walking back to disappear into the kitchen once more. Many believe these apparitions to be residual haunts like Rachel, but there have been many cases where one of the Harvey Girls will turn to give the stunned onlooker a quick smile and nod of the head in greeting before continuing on with their job at hand. This is simply not something a residual haunting would or could do. A lack of acknowledgement from one of these Harvey Girls could be one of two things: (1) the observer is in the formal dining room without being dressed in formal attire or (2) that the Harvey Girls were so good at their jobs that acknowledging someone they perceive to be a non-diner would take away their attention from those they are currently serving.

The Casa del Desierto is also known for the common types of paranormal happenings, the feeling of being watched and followed while inside the building; seeing shadows out of the corners of your eye, such as the blogger stated; and of course sudden cold spots in a room that had only moments before been a scorching hot sauna brought on by the desert sun.

The Casa del Desierto, also known as the Barstow Harvey House, was luckily saved from the wrecking ball as so many others of this historic chain were not. Others, like the El Graces in Needles, California, are still with us, albeit as a rent-for-event-only venue, and others still, such as La Posada in Winslow, Arizona, are still wonderful hotels and restaurants where one can sleep and dine in the atmosphere and style of the past. For those ParaTravelers road tripping along the Mother Road in California, a stop at the Barstow Harvey House is a must. Besides the spirits that reside here, the railroad museum has a great collection inside the museum proper and rail cars from many generations of rail history. If you miss either the inside of the Casa del Desierto or the rail museum, the one thing you shouldn't miss is the Route 66 Mother Road Museum. Here you will find photos of old Route 66 and Barstow, historic artifacts, books about the Mother Road and anything else a road tripper or ParaTraveler could possibly want. You won't be sorry you stopped in.

# 9

# ELMER'S BOTTLE TREE RANCH

*Some beautiful paths can't be discovered without getting lost.*
*—Erol Ozan*

The Mother Road has always been known for its kitschy roadside stops. Motor courts where one could sleep in a teepee, giants holding everything from rocket ships to wrenches and a swimming hole where one could slide off a blue whale's back, these and many other oddities all greeted travelers along Route 66. California was no exception to the whacky architecture, as a huge orange in the middle of the city of Fontana or the state's own teepee motor court, the Wigwam, can attest. But where most of these Mother Road attractions were built in the 1930s through the 1950s, there is one in California that is both new and well known, as well as spiritually inspired. I am talking about the now famous Elmer's Bottle Tree Ranch in the small burg of Oro Grande.

Elmer Long was born in 1947 to a father who loved to collect things. Old signs, pieces of furniture, ancient auto parts and things he would find just lying around that nobody wanted anymore. What his father collected most, and the thing that he seemed most mesmerized by, were bottles. It didn't matter what type of bottle, what color or size it was, the only thing it had to be was glass. When the family moved to the high desert country of California in 1970, more specifically, Oro Grande, Elmer's father found a whole new world of scavenging. Almost daily, Elmer and his dad would go out into the Mojave Desert looking for treasures. This was a perfect example

Elmer's Bottle Tree Ranch welcomes folks, free of charge, to look around and enjoy the unusual artworks.

of the old saying, "One man's trash is another man's treasure," and the Longs were finding many examples. And of course, if a bottle was found, it was picked up, placed in a bag and brought home.

As Elmer aged, he took on the trade of welder and eventually hired on with the local cement factory. As time went on, Elmer began to use his welding skills in a more artistic way. He would create little things at the factory using scrap, and when fixing things, he would come up with inventive yet practical ways to make the repairs. Elmer found that being creative and artistic made him happy. It also seemed to please those around him who noticed his work. Elmer not only practiced his art at work but also tinkered around the house, which amused his aging father. While they were scouring the desert, Elmer used to follow his dad around taking notes on what they found, and where, and now, his father followed Elmer around the house looking at what his son was up to in his creative endeavors. Life in the Mojave was treating the Longs well.

After Elmer's father passed away, Elmer inherited all of the family's belongings: the house, land and everything in his dad's strange collections of odds and ends, bits and pieces, and every last one of the hundreds and hundreds of bottles he had collected over the years. The bottle collection

You never know what you will come across at the Bottle Tree Ranch.

was extensive, as was everything else scavenged from the area. What does one do with a massive collection of bottles and scrap metal? Well, if you are a welder and artist, you turn them into artwork, but what can be produced with bottles and metal?

Elmer pondered what he could turn all of the collected paraphernalia into when he remembered a book he had read years earlier. The book dealt with superstitions, paganism, spiritualism and other types of metaphysical theory. One of the things that Elmer had always thought interesting was the old Appalachian and southern belief in what is called a bottle tree. Thinking about it, Elmer realized this was the perfect solution and art project for all of the bottles and bits that lay around his property. Once Elmer got an idea into his head, he wasn't one to let it linger, and he started his first project as soon as he got home from work. Elmer put up the first bottle tree in his front yard in 2000.

Once the tree was up, Elmer began to notice that folks driving by on Route 66 began to stop, back up and take a picture of his artwork. All day he watched as people parked their cars on either side of the road, snapping pictures of his bottle tree. They all seemed polite—most asked if it was OK to look and take pictures—and all complimented him on the unusual piece and his skill. Encouraged by the compliments and appreciation for his work, Elmer began to create more bottle trees. He would use all of the scrap metal he and his father had collected over the years, and he would sort the glass bottles and pick different ones for each tree so that not one of the bottle trees was alike. When Elmer retired, he began to create bottle trees full time. It is said that early on, Elmer walked out into his front yard when there were only a few bottle trees standing, and he was greeted by the beautiful rays of sunlight shining through the colored bottles. The haunting yet soothing sound of the wind made music as it was caught by the bottles.

Over time, Elmer created a veritable bottle tree forest in his front yard. Each tree was unusual, and each placed in an order that made it easy to walk past while still being close enough to see every detail. Those items that had been collected over the years but couldn't be used for a tree were placed artistically around the yard among the trees or hung on the fence. Elmer named his urban art museum Elmer's Bottle Tree Ranch and lived in the house on the property. The front yard was deep and large, so Elmer used this for his art, but he kept the backyard, which was also huge, as his private domain. His front porch became his workspace, and he also set up an area with a lounge chair and guest logbook where people could come, sign the book and chat with him as he relaxed in his recliner.

Elmer Long loved people. He would often be found strolling through his bottle forest, talking to folks, explaining his art, laughing and just enjoying the travelers' company. Elmer would often lament the fast pace of the world and how sad it was that people drove the "soulless" interstates and how they no longer enjoyed the slower pace of the old roads, discovering new people and the places they call home. Elmer, for one, found this a sad state of affairs for the lost joy that he believed travelers were giving up for speed. With this in mind, Elmer never charged for the privilege of wandering through his front yard wonderland but did provide a wooden wishing well, for those charitably inclined, along with a donation jar set at the table where he worked and entertained his visitors.

Elmer Long, the man with the long gray beard who many said looked like a band member from ZZ Top, passed away in June 2019 at the age of seventy-two. On that day, the Mother Road lost a true gentleman but one who left a legacy of beauty, both in sight and sound, as well as a dream that the world could return to a slower pace, where folks could meet their neighbors, enjoy a drink and chat and remember the America that once was.

Oro Grande is considered by many to be one of, if not the most haunted towns in California. From its cemetery and antique stores to its old service

Blue bottle trees are said to be the most effective in capturing evil spirits.

Many things are tossed out into the desert, and many find their way back to Elmer's yard.

stations, now lost motels and auto courts, Oro Grande is known for its ghosts. One place that one would think might be haunted, being on former Native American land and close to all of these other haunted hot spots, would be the Bottle Tree Ranch. As much as one would believe ghosts to be at Elmer's property, there has never been a single sighting there, and Elmer's art may be the reason that there never will be.

When Elmer came up with the idea for his Bottle Tree Ranch, it was because of a book about metaphysical and spiritual things he had read years before. As stated, his idea came from a long-held belief that bottle trees could contain spirits. Dating back to around the ninth century AD in the Congo region of Africa, bottle trees began to appear as a way to help ward off evil spirits. There is some debate about when bottles first began to be used; some say it was much earlier than the nineteenth century. Felder Rushing wrote in his book *Bottle Trees and Other Whimsical Glass Art* (St. Lynn's Press, 2013), "For years I subscribed to the common thread of lore that dates the origin of bottle trees to the Congo area of Africa…but after extensive research, I find that bottle trees and their lore go back much farther in time." Holy men would erect these trees, always with the bottles facing down. It was believed that evil spirits, demons, along with mean and angry ghosts would be drawn to the warmth of the bottles at night, becoming trapped until the sunrise when the rays of the newfound day would destroy them. Many scholars believe that the bottle tree is connected to the evolution of the witch bottle as protective magic.

When the African slave trade began, the new slaves brought their beliefs along with them, first to England and its colonies, then to other parts of Europe and finally to the Americas. After the United States was founded, its citizens and the people they enslaved began to spread out, and the legend of the bottle tree spread with them. Nowhere is the legend of the bottle trees more pronounced than in the Appalachia region and among the southern states, where African slaves were the most common. As the legend was retold, then retold again, many put their own spin on the tale. Some believe that to capture spirits and to ward off evil, one must hang the bottles from a tree with twine, others that they must be stuck right onto a tree's branches and others still that the tree must be created using the creator's own energy to activate the magic. One Hoodoo tradition states that a bottle tree must be created at a crossroads to work properly.

Whatever is believed about the different theories regarding the creation or what the proper placement of the bottles must be, all of them agree that the color of the bottle is important. Although any color can be used, including clear glass, a blue bottle is the most effective at capturing a wandering or threatening spirit. Another tenet that hasn't changed through the retellings is that when created, the bottle tree will lure in a spirit by the moonlight shining through the bottle; once captured, the entity cannot escape, once inside, the spirit is trapped. When the sun rises the next day, the entity is destroyed, once again allowing the bottle to trap its next spirit. It is said that the haunting sound of the wind passing over the mouth of the bottle is actually the trapped spirit crying out in torment.

Even today, when one drives through the southern half of the United States, one will pass by homes and businesses and see bottle trees placed in front yards and parkways to help ward off evil spirits. You can find the same while driving through the Appalachia region of the country. Most, if not all of these bottle trees will be made up of blue bottles. Many folks not only believe that the trees will protect them but also subscribe to the theory that blue bottles will also help to bring good luck and prosperity to their lives, a good luck charm if you will.

Keeping the legends of the bottle tree in mind, one can see how a site with so many in one place can help keep ghosts away from the location, even in a town as haunted as Oro Grande, and keep any bad juju as far away

From mundane items, such as typewriters, to firearms and automobiles, the desert's trash was Elmer's treasure.

as possible from that many traps. Whether you believe in the bottle tree as a ward against evil and angry spirits, or if you just love art in the form of arranged junk, Elmer's Bottle Tree Ranch is a place that must be seen to understand. While there, just remember Elmer's advice to slow down your life and see the wonder that surrounds you. When you merge back onto the Mother Road, don't turn toward the interstate; instead, turn back into America and the beauty it holds.

# 10

# ORO GRANDE

*Because the greatest part of a road trip isn't arriving at your destination.
It's all the wild stuff that happens along the way.*
— *Emma Chase,* Tamed

Directly on Route 66 sits the small, almost forgotten town of Oro Grande. The town isn't much and never really was, but what it lacks in size, it more than makes up for in spirit. Only about five miles northeast of the town of Victorville and thirty-two miles west of Barstow, Oro Grande started out life as Lane's Crossing, when, in 1859, Aaron G. Lane set up his homestead and supply stop catering to expeditions and settlers moving through the area along the nearby Mojave River. Lane sold his ranch in 1865 and moved downriver, where, in 1873 a rich ore strike was found worth about $160 in gold and $18 in silver per ton. This was just east of Lane's new ranch.

The new find led to the organization of the Sliver Mining District, and in 1880, a new strike a few miles away signaled the beginning of the Red Mountain Gold District. With numerous claims being filed, a new town arose, with the first post office being opened in 1881, named Halleck. The name came from the gold mine and stamp mill that had been set up; its chemist, a Mr. Halleck, was well liked. The two mining districts were combined into the Oro Grande Mining District. The name Halleck lasted until 1927, when the name of the town was changed to the one we know today, Oro Grande, meaning *large gold*.

Oro Grande is a fading town, but being directly on the Mother Road, it is hanging on by a thread.

As the gold and silver began to play out, other commodities took their place. Limestone being the main mineral coming out of the new mines and one of the key ingredients in producing cement, Oro Grande became a prime supplier of cement in the state. Having a modern stamp mill, the mines at Calico a few miles to the east shipped their ore to the town for processing, and this helped bring in much needed capital to the town as the gold and silver began to wane. Although Calico built stamp mills in the town of Daggett, which was much closer, and their own mills at the town, some shipments still made their way to Oro Grande, helping to keep the town alive.

By the time Route 66 came directly through the town of Oro Grande, the Riverside Cement factory was already in full swing; because of this, Oro Grande played a big part in the Mother Road's construction. Cement from the factory was widely used in building the road, and with Oro Grande having a much-needed supply, Route 66 was planned to run right through the town itself. The route spurred shops, stores and service stations to pop up along the road from Helendale to Victorville, and Oro Grande became home to one of the first Mohawk gas stations in the western Mojave Desert. Two motels, the Paradise Inn and the simply named Motor Inn, along with

Pinky's Service Station (La Delta Service Station and Auto Court) were also added.

When a man by the name of Benjamin "Bugsy" Siegel completed his mob-funded Flamingo Hotel and Casino in the late 1940s, Las Vegas, which had always been a gambling town, began to grow as more and more folks made their way to the glitz and neon of the Nevada desert city. Adults looking to get away from their kids and jobs for a weekend or perhaps longer were driving to Las Vegas, and Hollywood celebrities were flocking to the town to stay in the posh suites. Those same celebrities would perform on the stages that many of the new casinos were installing so their guests wouldn't have to leave the casinos, or the tables, to see a show. As the popularity of Las Vegas skyrocketed, stars like Dean Martin, Sammy Davis Jr. and even Old Blue Eyes, Frank Sinatra, would pass through Oro Grande. Many of these stars stopped for fuel, food and, on occasion, for the night in one of the town's small inns. It looked as if the small town of Oro Grande had come into its own and was on its way to growth.

As is the norm with most of old Route 66, growth was not to be, as the Federal Highway Bureau and the needs of the average driver had other plans for the many stops, towns and service stations along the Mother Road. US 40 had already been replacing Route 66 from Oklahoma through the Golden State, and where this interstate ended in Barstow, California, it merged into Interstate 15, which continued on to San Diego heading southwest and Las Vegas and beyond going east. Where Interstate 40 was killing towns along Route 66 in Arizona, Texas, Oklahoma and eastern California, Interstate 15 was doing the same in California, from Barstow to Santa Monica. While San Bernardino, west to the Pacific Ocean, was able to stay alive due to its urban influence even though Interstate 10 was slowing traffic on the Mother Road, the desert towns suffered extreme hardships for lack of traffic that had once streamed through their towns.

Barstow was saved much of the economic downfall due to the city being an important railroad crossing and a place where travelers stopped before heading on to Las Vegas or Laughlin, Nevada; almost all of the other small towns suffered severe hardships or complete ruin. Today, most of the small towns east of Barstow that were once thriving communities are nothing more than memories or ghost towns decaying in the harsh sun of the Mojave Desert. Others, like Goffs and Amboy, are hanging on by sheer will in the hope that they can be revived as nostalgic remnants of days gone by with the newfound interest in and travel along the Mother Road. Others have been reduced to nothing more than living ghost towns, kept barely alive because

Many of the businesses in Oro Grande are now nothing more than shells of what they once were.

of other economic reasons, like the cement plants of Oro Grande and the many spirits that inhabit the town. You see, Oro Grande is said to have the oldest and most haunted cemetery in San Bernardino County, in addition to being the most haunted town in the Mojave Desert itself.

Oro Grande Historic Memorial Park is thought to have had its first burial around the same time the town was founded in 1852 as a trading post. It is hard to tell exactly when, because records from the time were not kept, and many of the grave markers are nothing more than blank white crosses. A majority of the more than 132 graves here are those of miners or cement workers; however, there are others who have been interred here over the years. It is said that there are many unmarked graves in the Oro Grande cemetery and that even before settlers arrived it was a burial ground for the Native Americans in the area. With so many unmarked graves; graves with crosses that have no names, dates or information on who is buried under them; and the possible untold number of Native Americans buried here, it should come as no surprise that this cemetery is said to be quite haunted.

While attending the annual Oro Grande Days festival, I had the pleasure of meeting Joe Manners. Joe was the unofficial mayor at the time of my visit to Oro Grande, and he is a town historian and the cemetery's caretaker.

Joe met me at the gates of the graveyard—incidentally, his house is only steps away from the burial ground—and began telling me about all of the different paranormal goings-on that have occurred here. He began by explaining that not all of the ghosts have remained in the cemetery but have been visiting the homes surrounding it. Even Joe's own house has had quite a few spirits come to call.

Joe told me that there is one room in his home that neither he nor any visitors can or will stay in overnight. He said that people see shadows walking in the room, will feel a sense of unease the moment they enter, and will constantly be awakened throughout the night. He told me that a sliding door used to open on its own, and every time he closed it, a few minutes later the door would open again.

One of the first Mohawk Service Stations in California. As Oro Grande's fortunes receded, so did the need for this iconic relic of the past.

After this happened a few times, he called out to whatever spirit was doing it to stop, and it didn't happen again. Joe believes that one of the spirits in his house is that of a cowboy. He believes this because one time he spotted what looked like a man walking through his home and out through the wall. The figure was wearing a long coat, like a duster, and sporting a cowboy hat. At other times, overhead lights and other things hanging in his home will begin swinging for no reason and then stop just as suddenly. He said these same occurrences also happen in most of the other homes near the cemetery.

According to Joe, there is a house near him but a bit closer to the cemetery where the folks have a shed. This family set up a play area in a section of the shed for their kids, but the children won't go anywhere near the shack. According to the children, they have seen the figure of a woman going into the shed, but not through the open door. It would seem that when the kids see her enter the small building, it is by passing through the closed door. Other odd things that seem to happen in the neighborhood of the Oro Grande Cemetery are lights going on and off, cabinet drawers opening and closing of their own volition and doors opening and then slamming shut when no one is near them. It appears that living near the cemetery offers a bit of the unexpected to the adventurous, yet most now give no thought to the goings-on.

Within the cemetery itself, there are quite a few spirits that are seen—and often. Joe not only gives ghost tours of the graveyard but also allows investigators the opportunity to come in and investigate the location for a small donation toward its upkeep. Inside the graveyard, one will find the ghost of a little girl who hangs around one of the crosses. This cross has no names or dates on it, so no one is sure who is buried in the grave, so it is possible that this child was laid to rest here—either her or the small boy that is seen peering through her legs and hiding behind her. The way the boy clings to the girl, many assume that it may be her younger brother. This unmarked grave may be the boy's and not the girl's, or if they were brother and sister and passed away at the same time, from a pandemic or accident, they could possibly both be interred here.

These same children may be the young boy and girl who are often seen running around the cemetery playing with each other. If this is the case, it is not unusual for them to be seen hiding one minute, then cavorting around the graveyard in play the next. Maybe they are just trying to figure out the newcomers' intentions before trusting them enough to play near them. Another area where kids have been seen is near the graves of two teenagers who were struck and killed by a train in 1939. Being along the Santa Fe Railroad tracks, as much of Route 66 is, and with many freight trains

The little girl in this photo from the 1800s is said to be the child who haunts the antique shop.

passing through daily on their way to and from the Riverside Cement Plant, it is a wonder that more people haven't been struck in the past. These kids will often be seen standing near the back of the cemetery or, on occasion, simply watching those touring the graveyard. Joe mentioned that once, while visitors were looking at the graves of the two teenagers killed by the train, Tony and Maddy by name, a nearby train whistle sounded, and the folks immediately heard two young voices cry out, "Quick, the train's coming. Run!" and then silence. The voices came from next to the graves of the kids, and these folks were the only ones in or near the cemetery at the time.

The Oro Grande Cemetery is just across the tracks from Route 66, but as you drive down the Mother Road you will see a smattering of shops and stores bordering the road. Many of these are well known in town as having their own resident spirits, and none more than Antique Station and All Aboard Antiques, which share the same long building. Employees of the Antique Station, on the northeast side of the building, told me that they have a little girl that haunts the store and likes to close the bathroom door and hold it shut while folks are using it. When not engaged in playing these pranks, she will sometimes be seen just hanging out in the loo, which can be a bit disturbing for the gentlemen customers. Other times, this child will be seen wandering around the store both in the upper area and the lower section of the store, which leads to and is connected to the other shop, All Aboard. Many who have seen her say that she will give them a smile and then go about her playing or browsing. The child is known to move boxes around, and on occasion, one will hear small footsteps following them, but when one turns to look, there is no one there. There is a photograph hanging on the wall behind the cash register of Antique Station from the mid-1800s. It shows a group of people standing in the building, and one of these folks is a little girl around eight years old. Those who have seen the ghost child say that the girl in the picture is the spirit that haunts the store. They say there is no mistaking the dress, bow or hairstyle between the photo and the young spirit. This child gives one the feeling of friendliness and ease.

At the time of this writing, this antique shop had a wedding dress on display for sale. Over the time that the dress has been on display, many folks have approached the employees saying they can feel a strange energy coming from the dress. They say that it gets stronger as one nears the display and recedes as you move away. This has happened on so many occasions since the wedding dress has been in the shop that no one can deny it. One day a psychic came into the shop and mentioned that a woman, who had been married in the building long before it was a store, was hanging around

This wedding dress is said to have the bride's spirit attached to it, and it is believed that once the dress is sold, the ghostly bride will leave with the dress.

the dress. She said the woman was attached to it and would most likely leave when the dress was sold.

In the lower area of the building is All Aboard Antiques. Here, I was told that a six-foot-tall shadow or shadow person is often seen near the area of the cash register, although he has been seen in other areas. Once, when carrying in some furniture, a man saw this spirit dart in front of him heading to his right into the upper section of the shop. To say that the apparition startled him would be an understatement, but when he saw the same figure a month later on the stairs, where he had seen it before, he realized that the spirit was most likely not harmful. He did go on to say that he hoped he wouldn't see it again regardless of the ghost's intentions. This section of the building was once a tractor hauling company, and the owners and employees believe this shadow figure may have been someone killed in a tractor accident.

The upper areas of All Aboard Antiques are actually a series of small, open rooms, each with its own period items displayed. In one of these rooms there seems to be a spirit that will open all of the closed cabinet doors and drawers and close all of the ones that should remain open. This has been done in full view of both customers and employees alike. The first time that this was witnessed was around 6:30 p.m., well after the store had closed, and it frightened the employee to the point they almost quit. This employee has now become accustomed to it and merely finds it amusing. In this same room, and also in front of customers, things will begin to simply move on their own. A glass will slide along the top of its display case, a book will slip out of a bookcase and drop to the floor or a piece of clothing will fall off its rack when a customer passes by.

One day a couple and their daughter came into the store to look around and shop. After a while, the man became annoyed at his wife and daughter because the girl was running up and down the aisles and his wife wasn't stopping her. He was trying to look at an item and was perturbed that he had to stop what he was doing and calm his child down before she broke something. The next time he saw his daughter dart past, he yelled at her to stop running and turned in her direction. When he looked, he couldn't spot her anywhere and couldn't see his wife either. A few moments later, he spotted both of them far away and heading back from the restroom in the other store. He found out that they had both gone to Antique Station and the restroom more than twenty minutes earlier. There were no other children in either store, and he had been alone the entire time he was becoming annoyed with his daughter.

The owner of All Aboard told me that one day while she was sitting at the front desk doing office work and waiting on customers, she felt the back of her hair being pulled. She said that from the way it was tugged and the playful manner in which it was done it seemed as if it was a child just having a bit of fun. She told me that she has never seen the little girl from Antique Station come into her section of the building, but with what occurred with the gentleman thinking his daughter was running amok and her own hair being playfully tugged, she couldn't rule out the possibility that the child was playing in the All Aboard Antique Store as well.

The Oro Grande Cemetery is said to be the oldest cemetery in San Bernardino County, and it may also be the most haunted.

The Cross-Eyed Cow Pizza Parlor, which many say has the best pizza in San Bernardino County, seems to have a couple of ghosts that would agree. It is not unheard of that employees closing up for the night watch as the back door opens and closes on its own. Even when they don't actually see the door moving, they will hear the sound of the cowbell attached to the door sound as if someone is coming in, only to find out that no one is there. Employees have also reported seeing numerous shadow figures walking around the dining room and have heard the sounds of people, seemingly ordering food when the restaurant is completely empty. If the spirits in Oro Grande come back just for the pizza, who are we to argue about it being the best pizza around?

Another antique store that is said to be haunted, albeit not by the owner, is Shelley's Shop Around the Corner. While talking to Shelley, she told me that on occasion, they will see spectral dogs and cats about the store and the yard. She went on to say that this doesn't mean the store is haunted, only that the animals feel comfortable there. Shelley went on to say that there is no activity in the store, besides the animals, and that she is not a believer in the paranormal. When talking to "Mayor" Joe, however, who has a deep connection to Shelley and the store, he said the shop is most definitely haunted. Joe said that on many occasions as he was opening up the antique shop, they would find items that had been right where they were supposed to be, now stacked neatly on the floor. At other times, they will find things moved from their place during working hours, even though no one has come into the shop who could have moved the items. Joe finds Shelley's denial of spirit activity quite amusing given the amount of activity that goes on at the antique store.

One other spirit that Joe Manners mentioned—and one that he claims has been seen by everyone who lives and works in Oro Grande—is a spirit they named the Lady in White. It seems that most places that are haunted have their own lady in white, and Oro Grande is no different. No one knows who this lady is, and she has derived the name because of the fancy white dress she is always seen wearing. This woman is always glimpsed walking down the sidewalk of Route 66 as if going about her daily business. When visiting Oro Grande, a must for Mother Road aficionados, and ParaTravelers alike, make sure to ask those in town about their encounters with this classy Lady in White or the many other experiences they may have had while living and working in this haunted Route 66 town.

# 11

# THE AZTEC HOTEL

*Afoot and lighthearted I take to the open road, healthy, free, the world before me.*
—*Walt Whitman*

Not many people have heard of the city of Monrovia, but mention the Aztec Hotel and watch recognition come over their faces. For Route 66 aficionados, a smile always accompanies that recognition. The Aztec Hotel has made a name for itself among road trippers along the Mother Road, and you will be hard-pressed to find one who has not heard about this once grand relic of the early days of Route 66. What most of them are not aware of, however, is that the Aztec Hotel today may be more famous for its ghosts rather than its Art Deco and Mayan Revival architecture.

In 1924, the City of Monrovia, wanting to bring attention to the small town in the shadow of the great Los Angeles metropolis, decided that a grand hotel was just the thing to get people's attention and bring them to the city. With the chamber of commerce leading the way by selling stock in a hotel that hadn't even been designed yet, city leaders managed to raise $138,000 for the project, a tidy sum for that period. The city used part of the money to commission architect Robert Stacy-Judd to design and build a destination hotel, but his first design, a pre-Columbian cliff dwelling in Monrovia's Gold Hills, was flatly refused. However, Stacy-Judd's scaled-down, thirty-six-room Mayan Revival hotel, with an additional eight apartments and ground-floor retail space was accepted. Now all that was needed was a location. They decided that the main thoroughfare through

The Aztec Hotel is the last example of Mayan Revival architecture in the country.

Monrovia leading into Pasadena would be the most visible, and so, the Aztec Hotel was built on what would become Foothill Boulevard and Route 66.

Even though the Aztec Hotel is patterned after Mayan architecture, Stacy-Judd figured that no one really knew who or what Mayans were, and although Mayans were relatively unknown, the Aztecs were not. Knowing that the Aztec and Mayan cultures were almost interchangeable to modern Americans and from the same region, Stacy-Judd named his new venture the Aztec Hotel. With Stacy-Judd's signature triangular forms around the doorways and sides of the building, along with distinctive Art Deco flourishes mixed with Toltec, Mayan and Aztec flair, the hotel was hard to miss when driving through the city. The inside of the Aztec Hotel had an even more pronounced Mesoamerican style, but with the attention to detail for which Stacy-Judd was known, the Aztec Hotel gained a sordid reputation. With the interior adorned with scenes of the sun god, replete with human blood sacrifice, the god of lust and other artworks deemed "promiscuous"—at least for those times—many religious and women's groups refused to stay at the hotel and protested its existence.

When the Aztec Hotel opened in September 1925, it not only had thirty-six well-appointed guest rooms but also offered a supper club, dance hall and retail shops, including a coffee shop for those just passing by. Another thing the Aztec Hotel offered—it was now the height of the Prohibition era—was a basement speakeasy. It is also rumored that the apartments and one or two of the hotel rooms were used as a brothel to serve those coming to the speakeasy. Having this type of establishment in the basement also drew a somewhat unsavory element to the hotel, and when Route 66 came through in 1926, families, travelers and, for a brief time, migrants fleeing the Dust Bowl began to frequent the hotel. With all that was going on in the country, and along Route 66, the Aztec Hotel gained almost instant fame. Unfortunately, when the alignment of Route 66 through Monrovia was changed in 1931, it completely bypassed the hotel, and the Aztec began a swift and steady decline.

The Hollywood elite were coming to the Aztec Hotel to drink, party and be seen, but even prominent stars such as Tom Mix, Clark Gable and Bing Crosby couldn't save the Aztec from decline. As the Hollywood crowd evaporated, the Aztec became a boardinghouse and hangout for prostitutes, finally becoming a flophouse. Over time, Monrovia itself became an area of drug addicts, hookers, gangs and homeless, and the famous Aztec Hotel declined along with the city. Despite the unknown fate of this historic

The ornate lobby of the Aztec Hotel harkens back to the glitz and glamour of the hotel's Hollywood connection.

landmark, or maybe because of the uncertainty, the Aztec Hotel was listed on the National Register of Historical Places in 1978. Even with this designation, the fortunes of one of the last Mayan Revival structures in the country was still unclear.

The City of Monrovia, always conscious of preserving its history, embarked on an ambitious redevelopment project in the late 1970s, and by the early 1980s, Monrovia had kicked out the drug crowd, gangs and criminal element that had plagued the city and the Aztec Hotel. In 1983, the hotel's old restaurant and bar reopened as the Brass Elephant. The hotel was still used as low-income housing, and the restaurant had some business, but the Aztec Hotel suffered from economic hardships. In the late 1990s, the hotel was purchased by Kathie Reece with the idea of bringing the Aztec back to its former glory. With an endowment from the National Park Service, Reece began a careful restoration of the hotel and restaurant, but by 2012, the Aztec had once again gone through foreclosure and been put up for auction. Within three weeks, Qin Han Chen bought the Aztec Hotel, closed the entire property and began renovations.

Chen has been doing the renovations ever since he closed the Aztec Hotel. Some of the repairs, like the new guest room doors, weren't period accurate, and because the property is a historic Route 66 landmark, all modern improvements must replicate the original attributes of the property. The city's Historic Preservation Commission gave Chen two years to replace the modern-looking doors, but after Chen appealed to the city council, they told him that if he agreed to repair all of the neon signs, replace guest room windows on both the east and south sides of the building and construct a low protective wall along the roof called a parapet, they would agree to his request. As of this writing, the Aztec Hotel is still not open for overnight guests, but the owner hopes to begin taking reservations in the near future. Until then, the spirits of the Aztec Hotel will just have to content themselves with the patrons of the Mayan Bar and Grill, which shares the property. For you see, the Aztec Hotel may be one of the most haunted hotels along the entire route.

With its long history of shady characters, prostitution, gambling and a clientele of a dubious nature during the Aztec's speakeasy days, it isn't hard to believe that this Mayan Revival masterpiece has its fair share of ghostly guests. Even the *Los Angeles Times* admitted to the many spirits still "living" at this Route 66 original.

In a March 2001 article, the *Times* wrote, "For architectural historians, the Aztec is a gem, listed on the National Register of Historic Places. But its other fans include psychics and mediums, who are enthralled by a hotel where some guests may never have checked out." The paper claims that there are at least a dozen spirits that call the hotel home. It goes on to say that the most active spirit is that of a hooker who calls herself Razzle Dazzle. This Kansas-born call girl is said to have dark hair, worn in the 1920s finger-wave style, and carries a long cigarette holder that is symbolic of the Roaring Twenties. The paper says that the woman and a john retired to her room, 120, and began arguing over her price. The man apparently shoved Razzle Dazzle, who fell, struck her head and died. There is some speculation over this story, which we will get to later.

The paper writes that a psychic told the reporter that she could see many customers in evening clothes having a good time, laughing, drinking and dancing to the music of a Black piano player who is obscured by heavy cigarette and cigar smoke. The psychic stated that she was led to a room where a lot of money had been laundered and that the Jazz Age bookkeeper for the hotel led her to this room and others with paranormal significance.

In the ornate lobby of the hotel, just opposite the front desk, is the women's restroom. Before the hotel closed, many ladies using this loo claimed to have the doors swing open as they were using the stall, even though the door was securely latched. Voices were reported in the restroom, with some claiming to have their names called out as they were freshening up in front of the mirror and, in a few rare cases, seeing a deathly pale face staring at them over their shoulder. Of course, when they turn to look, no one is there. Even today, those touring the hotel will catch glimpses of wispy shadows in the hallways or lobby and even on the patio. These figures will be visible for only a second and then be gone as quickly as they appeared. It is believed that many of these figures may be the spirits of the women who worked at the brothel.

A paranormal group that investigated the Aztec in 2004 claimed that the room in the basement known as the "Green Room" held a portal that acted as a doorway for spirits to come into the hotel. The room received the nickname due to its green carpet and was one of the rooms used during the Aztec's speakeasy days. Those working at the hotel over the years claimed to have heard voices and unusual sounds in this room, including the sound of a growling dog. They also claimed to have found a Bible and several unused candles during the initial cleaning for the restoration.

Some of these stories have been confirmed; others seem to have been dispelled. But one thing is certain, after speaking with current Mayan Bar and Grill manager Willie Flores, who is also advising and working with the

*Left*: Attention to detail was paramount when designing the Aztec, so much so that even the foyer of the women's restroom was given a Mayan flair.

*Below*: The VIP room, even with its posh appointments, is said to have several ghosts that make themselves known.

owners to get the hotel back up and running, the Aztec Hotel is indeed haunted. While on one of my visits to the hotel, Willie gave me and my friend Louis Montero a tour of the Aztec. Willie is a great tour guide and told us about the rooms he led us to as well as the paranormal activity that he and his coworkers experienced in each room.

While leading us through the VIP room, Willie said that just after he hired on at the Mayan Bar, he was walking through this room and began hearing whistles. After looking around and seeing no one nearby, he continued on his way thinking it must have just been an echo coming from the street or parking lot. He heard the same whistles as he was walking back through when done with his errand. After the same thing happened a few more times, he realized that it could not be a coincidence, and then, when he heard the whistle close to his ear, he asked whoever was doing it to please stop, and he never heard the whistles again. However, his coworkers did. Another incident that took place early in Willie's career was when he was in the lobby and noticed a man sit down in a chair that had been placed between the VIP room and the hotel lobby by one of the staff. Willie said the man had black hair and was wearing black pants and a green shirt. Thinking that the gentleman was waiting for the bar manager, Willie went and told her someone was waiting. Confused, the manager, with Willie in tow, went back to the lobby, but the man was nowhere to be found. The manager mentioned the hotel ghosts to Willie, and since then, he keeps a tablecloth over the chair in the hopes that he won't see the spirit again.

About four months after being hired, Willie was sent to the walk-in cooler to get a case of beer. It was about 10:30 p.m., and even though the bar had a few patrons on the patio, the VIP room was empty. Leaving the cooler after getting the beer, Willie began to feel as if someone was watching him. As he continued to walk out to the patio bar, his head began to ache, and his legs began to feel heavy. When he was near the center of the room, he felt someone come up behind him and push him. Looking around, Willie saw that there was nobody there but was sure he had been shoved. Once he got back to the bar, he told the bartender not to ask him to go back to the cooler because he would have to refuse the order. Another time, he was working in the section of the Aztec where the apartments are located and began hearing someone calling his name. It sounded to him like whoever was calling out was far away. No one was living in the apartments at the time, and he and the manager, who was working in the office behind the front desk, were the only ones there, so he figured she was the one calling him. When he went up to her and asked what she wanted, she told him that it hadn't been her. This wouldn't be the last time Willie would hear his name called by one of the spirits.

While taking us up to the hotel rooms, Willie did mention that spirits have been seen in the hallways but said that they are more like shadows of people rather that solid apparitions. He said that it is almost impossible to tell the gender of the ghosts, but the speculation about them being prostitutes has only been put forth by psychics, some of whom he called "dubious." He did take us into room 120, which has been renumbered for obvious reasons, and told us that no one really knows what happened or if it was actually someone named Razzle Dazzle killed in the room. He said that another story that comes from room 120 is that of a man and his wife who were having an argument, and the wife accidentally hit her head and died. Another tale has it that a prostitute, perhaps Razzle Dazzle, after finishing up with her john, waited for him to fall asleep and then tried to rob him. When the man woke up and caught her, they wrestled and the woman hit her head on the radiator and died. When asked about another story relating to the other rooms nearby, whose radiators haven't worked since the night Razzle Dazzle died, he said he had never heard that story and that the other rooms' radiators worked just fine.

Willie did mention the "portal" in what he called the "Green Carpet Room" but couldn't confirm the validity of the claim, as he had only heard it from those who originally said it. He did say that he never noticed any unusually high activity in the room. He did mention that the Aztec Hotel did have tunnels running under it. He said these were used whenever the hotel was being raided by police so that those in the basement speakeasy could escape before being caught. He went on to say that at times, even though the tunnels are now closed off, it is not unusual to hear the sounds of talking and footfalls in certain areas behind the basement walls. It is believed that this is where the tunnel entrances were.

Willie said that the area where the apartments are located does have some activity, although minor, but that there is one room in this area that gives him a sense of calm and peace. Willie says that when he is in this room, he feels that nothing bad can happen to him. Willie now feels, if not comfortable with the spirits of the hotel, at least tolerant of them. He says that other than the one push he received early in his career, nothing violent or bad has ever occurred because of the ghosts. He thinks that they are just there, going about their business and having a bit of fun now and again with staff and guests.

The patio of the Aztec Hotel is now part of the Mayan Bar and Grill, but everywhere you look, you will see the artwork and murals of the hotel that still remain.

Even though the Aztec Hotel is not yet welcoming overnight guests, the Mayan Bar and Grill is open to serve you good food and classic drinks. So if you want to visit this historic slice of Route 66, come and enjoy a cocktail on the patio or food and appetizers in the bar while surrounded by beautiful Art Deco façades and Mayan Revival décor. Just don't be surprised if you see a few folks who seem to be from a different era who are enjoying the Aztec Hotel right along with you.

# 12
# THE PASADENA PLAYHOUSE

*Fill your life with experiences, not things. Have stories to tell, not stuff to show.*
*—unknown*

Just a block off Colorado Boulevard (Route 66) sits the Pasadena Playhouse. This icon of days gone by still hosts shows and events that make people laugh, cry, stare in wonder and sing along to their favorite songs and show tunes. From its beginnings in the early days of the twentieth century through rough times when it looked like the end for the old theater, the playhouse has endured, thrived and amused all walks of life. The theater has a loyal following of guests, and these include a number of spirits that have stayed on to both entertain and greet the patrons of the stage.

The "State Theater of California" had its beginnings in 1917, when Gilmor Brown and his troupe settled into the then small town of Pasadena. At the time, Pasadena was nothing more than a farming town where wealthy vacationers came to relax in the California sunshine and hike the beautiful Santa Monica Mountains. Gilmor set up his troupe in an old burlesque house, where, after rent and other costs, he had just enough to pay his actors, with some left over for himself that they all had a comfortable, if not lavish lifestyle. In the ten years they performed in the town, Gilmor and his performers' professionalism was such that Pasadena fell in love with the players, and the locals raised money through donations to move the troupe into the newly constructed Pasadena Community Playhouse in 1924. With its non-professional beginnings, the huge support of the community and the fact that it was the largest and most technically advanced venue west of the Mississippi, George Bernard Shaw likened it to the ancient festival of Dionysia and dubbed it the "Athens of the West." In 1937, the California legislature, being fans of the playhouse, unanimously voted the Pasadena Playhouse as the official State Theater of California.

During the theater's first forty years, it was the first American theater to stage all thirty-seven of Shakespeare's plays and would present almost five hundred world premieres, many by notable playwrights such as Tennessee Williams, Noël Coward and F. Scott Fitzgerald. Gilmor Brown, wanting to teach others the fine points of performing, opened the College of Theater Arts at the Pasadena Playhouse

The Pasadena Playhouse is the official state theater of California.

in 1928. By 1930, the school was being touted as "Hollywood's talent factory." Through the years, such talents as Charles Bronson, Dustin Hoffman, Raymond Burr, Gene Hackman, Ernest Borgnine, Mako and Sally Struthers have learned the art of performing in front of an audience. Later, as TV blossomed, a studio was opened to train writers, actors, directors and technicians the ways of television. One actor who got his big break while performing at the playhouse was *Superman* TV star George Reeves, and many believe that Reeves has never left the theater that he loved. The Pasadena Playhouse was becoming one of the premier theaters in the country.

When Gilmor Brown died in 1960, the theater slowly began a steady decline. By 1969, with colleges and universities expanding their drama departments and New York opening schools on Broadway, the School of Theater Arts closed down, and a few months later the theater filed for bankruptcy. The official Theater of California sat vacant, collecting dust until 1975, when the City of Pasadena stepped in and purchased the playhouse with the intent of restoring it to its past glory. It would take another few years, however, for the city to open the theater. With a grant from the Economic Development Administration, the city, with the assistance of real estate developer David G. Houk, who had matched the grant funds that

This reception room in Gilmor Brown's office is said to be haunted by Gilmor Brown himself and *Superman* star George Reeves.

the federal government required, the old Pasadena Playhouse was once again ready for an audience in 1982. It would take a few years for the main theater to reopen, but at least the playhouse was once again able to provide a scheduled season in the 99-seat "interim" balcony theater.

Today, the Pasadena Playhouse has been added to the National Register of Historic Places, and with the grand reopening of the main theater in 1986, the playhouse has become a leader in the theater community. Its 680-seat main venue has a year-round season of six plays, with more than three hundred performances each year. The smaller, more intimate stage hosts shows of both local and larger interest. Special performances, galas and Hollywood events are held at the theater, with many big-name celebrities performing in and viewing the many shows. The Hollywood elite are still coming to the Pasadena Playhouse today, but many of the past stars, crew and troupe players never left.

Over the years that the Pasadena Playhouse has been running shows, reports of paranormal activity have flooded in. So prevalent are the reports that the playhouse allows periodic, private paranormal investigations to be booked. To the historians and board members of the playhouse, this is just another opportunity to learn about the venue's history and to make a bit of money to help keep the theater's continuing restoration going strong.

One of the most talked about spirits haunting the Pasadena Playhouse began shortly after the man's death in 1959. This man had a long career in TV and movies, beginning in the 1930s with a part in the film *Gone with the Wind* and continuing up to his death with his starring role in the TV series *The Adventures of Superman*. I am speaking of the incomparable George Reeves.

Most people would look at George Reeves's life as a fairy tale, but sometimes, for those involved, that fairy tale can be rife with disappointment that others could not see. Such was the case with Mr. Reeves. Reeves began acting while in high school and split his time between the stage and the school boxing team. While in junior college, Reeves started trying out for parts at the Pasadena Playhouse, where he then got his start in professional acting. Reeves's talent eventually landed him a roll in the epic movie *Gone with the Wind*, for which he received great acclaim (his movie credit is listed under the wrong character). It seemed that George Reeves was destined for a stellar movie career.

After performing in recruitment films for the military during World War II, Reeves appeared in a few B movies and was cast in the starring role of a TV serial, which lasted for only fifteen episodes before cancellation. After performing on Broadway for a few years and a failed marriage, Reeves decided to try out for a new TV series titled *The Adventures of Superman* as a way to get both his name and talent in front of Hollywood producers and directors in the hopes of gaining more movie roles. Unfortunately, this was not the case, as he was now typecast. After a strange Hollywood affair, a career stalled by his most famous role and a deep depression, George Reeves was found dead by an apparently self-inflicted gunshot wound on June 15, 1959. His death is still mired in controversy to this day. (For more information on Reeves, read *Hollywood Obscura: Death, Murder and the Paranormal Aftermath.* Schiffer Books, 2017)

Reeves has made himself known in the house where he died almost from the time of his burial. After his death, the house reverted to the woman he had been having an affair with and who was also one of the prime suspects in his rumored murder, Toni Mannix. Mannix was the wife of MGM Studio's general manager Eddie Mannix and had purchased Reeves's house for him. Not wanting to live in the house, Mannix rented it out but found that no one stayed long due to Reeves keeping them up at night. It wasn't just the home that Reeves returned to but the Pasadena Playhouse, a place that Reeves dearly loved.

George Reeves was well known for his sense of humor and playing pranks on his fellow actors at the playhouse. There are times when actors will have

The balcony in the main theater of the playhouse is said to occasionally have a spectral audience enjoying the show.

their makeup moved; it is usually found nearby, stacked up in ways almost like a Jenga puzzle. Other times, people will find that chair legs have been propped up so that if the unaware sits without looking, they will tip over. The stage crews will often find ropes tied into intricate knots but easy to untie, or tools will turn up missing only to be found propped up against their toolboxes. It was well known that Reeves thought of the Pasadena Playhouse as a second home. It would seem that he also thinks of the cast, crew and staff as family.

Another spirit that is well known at the playhouse is that of its creator, Gilmor Brown. Brown is also known to play practical jokes on those in the theater. Between Brown and Reeves, no one really knows which jokester is playing a trick on them at any given time. Brown has not been seen, that we know of, but when he is near, his presence can usually be felt. Brown has been sensed so often, along with Reeves, that one of the managers started to keep a journal of the activity at the playhouse. She has noted that personal objects, such as her own binoculars, have gone missing from the empty theater. Staff items have disappeared only to be found mere moments later by other employees, and doors have locked on their own just as a staff member tries to leave the playhouse. Many times, these same doors cannot be unlocked, prompting the employee to leave from another exit.

The Pasadena Playhouse will occasionally perform Sunday matinees. During one particular show, at the same time in each performance, the house lights would suddenly come on. The technicians could find nothing wrong with the wiring or switches or find any other explanation. This went on for a whole month until the production ended its run. These same technicians would come back after intermission to find their earphones rearranged in the booth, and on more than one occasion, the sound and lighting controls would be reset, necessitating hurried reconfiguring to the show's needs. All of this happened in an empty and locked control booth.

The balcony level of the playhouse is where Gilmore Brown's office is located. This area has been kept just the way Brown left it, with the furnishings, books and tables in the same spots Brown left them when he died. This was not only where Brown managed the day-to-day operations of the theater but also where he entertained his guests, and Gilmor Brown truly loved to entertain. Maybe this is why his office and parlor are well known haunts of Brown to this day.

The backstage area is known to have quite a bit of paranormal activity, although no one is sure who these spirits may be. Investigators have caught audio of both male and female voices in the changing and makeup rooms, and psychics have picked up feelings of both sadness and joy in most of the rooms in the playhouse. The ladies from the Paranormal Houses Wives paranormal group had been investigating the playhouse when one of their team members, Jennifer Storey Turner, had an experience she won't soon forget. Jennifer said that she can sometimes tell if a room or area is haunted when she gets a sudden onrush of feelings not her own. This is what happened during the investigation of the venue. She felt fine while in the theater change rooms and female shower room of the playhouse, but on entering the sewing/wardrobe room, all that changed. As Jennifer entered this room, a sudden wave of nausea overcame her. Hoping it would pass, she participated in trying to communicate with any spirits present but became more ill as time went by. When her teammate Erin Potter suddenly jumped up from being scratched by an invisible force, Jennifer decided to go out into the hallway rather than disturb her team by possibly throwing up. Once Jennifer was back in the hallway, however, she began to noticeably feel better. She said that it took her about ten minutes to stop being nauseated, and she was able to continue with the investigation—but did not go back into the wardrobe room. Jennifer said that the following day she woke up with a terrible hangover even though she hadn't had a drink the night before.

Gilmor Brown is often seen in the conference room of his office.

The Pasadena Playhouse is truly a magnificent and historic venue, one that any Route 66 ParaTraveler should consider going to see. As haunted as the theater may be, the spirits here seem to be more about joking around, having a good time and entertaining those seeking them out. Just remember, when visiting this official State Theater of California, you may not only see actors and actresses on stage but also Superman himself.

# 13

# COLORADO STREET (SUICIDE) BRIDGE

*To anyone out there who's hurting—it's not a sign of weakness to ask for help.*
*It's a sign of strength.*
*—Barack Obama*

Colorado Street Bridge, located in Pasadena, California, and once an important part of Route 66, has become known as the "Suicide Bridge" by most everyone in the Los Angeles area. Unfortunately, it earned that name by countless lost, broken and sad individuals throwing themselves from its lofty heights; city officials have had to erect an ugly but mostly functional suicide prevention chain-link fence.

When Pasadena was first incorporated in 1886, trying to reach the nearby city of Los Angeles was no easy task. Even though it was only eleven miles away, one had to traverse the Arroyo Seco, or seasonal river. This required descending a steep grade, crossing the river and then laboriously trekking up the other side. It was hard enough on foot, but if a wagon was in tow, laden with goods, it made the journey much harder and more perilous. To help make things a bit easier, J.W. Scoville built a wooden trestle span over the river in the late 1880s. This solved only one problem; people now had a way over the arroyo but still had to contend with the steep grades. As the twentieth century approached and automobiles began arriving on the scene, as hard as these grades were for horse-drawn wagons, they were almost impossible for early automobiles.

The Colorado Street Bridge is considered a masterpiece of architectural design.

By the early 1900s, with cars crossing the old wooden bridge and struggling with the hills, city officials had decided to build a span at street level over the Arroyo Seco and, in the process, extend Colorado Street. Pasadena hired engineer Joseph Waddell to design the span but ran into problems almost immediately on the start of construction. The sometimes-wet riverbed, along with the need to construct the bridge with a slight uphill eastward grade made solid footing a challenge, and ideas were needed to solve this drawback. Engineer John Mercereau solved the snag by curving the bridge fifty-two degrees at the center. When completed, the Colorado Street Bridge, with its Romanesque columns and arches, graceful curve, classical balusters and cast-iron, multi-globed lamp posts, was truly a work of art.

At 1,467 feet long and 150 feet high at its tallest point above the riverbed, the Colorado Street Bridge was hailed as the tallest and longest bridge in California at that time. When the span was opened to traffic on December 13, 1913, Pasadena residents hopped into their decorated newfangled automobiles and created an impromptu parade as they drove across the city's new landmark. Route 66 through Pasadena has a few different alignments depending on the years; however, from 1934 to 1936, the Colorado Street Bridge was very much a part of the Mother Road.

Drivers would pass over this span on their way to the historic terminus in downtown Los Angeles. It was during this time that the Colorado Street Bridge gained its nickname, the Suicide Bridge.

The first recorded suicide on the bridge took place on November 16, 1919, when seventy-year-old Smith Osgood threw himself from one of the alcoves along the highest point of the span. In his suicide note, Osgood wrote, "Please telephone GG Wheat, undertaker, Huntington Park, to send for my body and prepare for its cremation. I am about to make the leap from beautiful Colorado Street Bridge. Farewell, beautiful Pasadena! I loved you so well!" To this day, no one knows why Osgood took his own life, but his suicide seemed to open the floodgates of more to come.

During the Great Depression years, it is said that over fifty men and women took their lives on the bridge between 1929 and 1933. It is unclear what drew so many people to the Colorado Street Bridge to end their lives; maybe it was a cycle of one person seeing the news about a jumper and then getting the idea and so on and so on, but whatever the reason, by 1933, the bridge had earned its somber nickname.

Perhaps the saddest and most well-known suicide is that of a young mother thought to be named Myrtle Ward. Despondent over her husband's new, low-paying job and having to quit her employment to watch over their baby, Myrtle began to conjure up images of her family starving, homeless and destitute all due to their financial situation and the economic depression the country was living under. Although none of her worries was coming to fruition, Myrtle's mind told her it was just around the corner. In an act of apparent desperation, Myrtle drove herself and her three-year-old daughter to the Suicide Bridge, threw her child over the railing and then followed her into oblivion. The child survived after falling into a tall pepper tree, but her mother was so badly injured that she writhed in pain for two hours before she succumbed to her injuries. Later in life, Myrtle's daughter said that it was only by angelic intervention that she did not die when her mother tossed her from the bridge.

Over the intervening years, more people came to the bridge to seek a permanent solution to a temporary problem. It is said that well over 150 souls died by suicide off the span; 30 have taken place since 2010. Finally, the city installed anti-suicide fencing along the bridge, and although it does detract from the original beauty of the architecture, it has seriously slowed those seeking to do themselves harm. With the number of deaths associated with the Colorado Street Bridge, it may not come as a surprise that this work of engineering art is a place known by locals and visitors alike as an extremely haunted location.

The trees and bushes below the Suicide Bridge have saved a few lives, including a small child—unfortunately, not enough to keep the bridge from its grisly reputation.

The first ghost stories involving the bridge began almost from the day the span opened to traffic. There is a tale about a construction worker who fell to his death and landed in wet cement that had just been poured into its forms. Since the worker was dead and removing his body would result in the ruination of the fresh cement, he was left in the forms and became a permanent part of the bridge. It is claimed that he haunts the Colorado Street Bridge to this day. This is a familiar story that seems to pop up every time there is a ghost at a site where cement has been used; this story has become almost laughable. As far-fetched as this tale is, it does have a bit of truth to its telling.

On August 1, 1913, three men were working on the bridge when their scaffolding collapsed. One man, H. Collins, suffered only minor injuries in the fall and completely recovered; another man, John Visco, fell on the rocks in the creek bed and was killed instantly. The third man, Charles Johnson, did fall into wet cement. Alive, but seriously injured, the man was removed from the cement and taken to the hospital. Johnson ended up losing his right arm and leg in the accident but otherwise recovered.

It is said that just after the span's opening, and to this day, people have heard the sound of a man calling out to people crossing the bridge on foot,

Spirits are said to walk below the Suicide Bridge and call out to the living.

telling them to "Look out" and "Hurry and get off the bridge." It is believed that this person is John Visco, trying to warn people of the impending scaffolding collapse. Locals and visitors walking across the bridge have also reported seeing an apparition of a woman in a white gown leaping from a parapet. Just before the lady jumps, she glances over at the onlookers, leaps and then vanishes while in midair. Yet another spirit commonly seen by those walking along the bridge is that of a man wearing wire-rimmed glasses and a suit who simply wanders back and forth seemingly in a daze. This could be what is called a residual haunting, as there have been no reports of interaction with the living.

Many people, both in the daytime and at night, have heard what they say sounds like cries and moans coming from below the bridge in the canyon. Ghost hunters come from all over to investigate the area, and many say that the arroyo underneath the Colorado Street Bridge is more haunted than the span itself. Many investigators report hearing strange sounds coming from all around them, and even though nothing but vegetation can be seen, the sounds continue. Both ghost hunters and those living nearby have reported seeing wispy phantom forms walking among

A suicide fence has been installed along the walkway of the bridge, but it has only slowed the rate of those seeking their own deaths.

Family and friends remember their deceased loved ones by placing locks at the site where they left this mortal plain.

the trees, and many have also heard the sound of a woman screaming, which sounds like she is falling from the span above. The scream will always abruptly stop as it nears that creek bed; many believe this to be the sound of Myrtle as she plummets to the ground. Myrtle is also seen walking around the area where her broken body was found as if looking for something. It is believed that she is eternally looking for the child she lost, unaware that her baby survived and lived a full life.

There have been numerous reports of a gruff male voice being heard from among the trees and rocks below the bridge. The voice seems to be blaming a woman for something, although he is never specific in his claim, "It's her fault." It is believed that this spirit may be that of Charles Winkelman. It seems that Charles's wife had been cheating on him, and he'd had enough and drove with his wife to the Colorado Street Bridge with the idea of killing himself while she watched. When they arrived at the span, he dragged his wife out of the car to take her with him. She managed to fight off her husband, and he then threw himself over the railings. This happened in 1934, and his spirit has been wandering below the bridge ever since.

Suicide is never the answer to a problem. Life is precious, and there is nothing that can't be overcome with time and patience. If any of my readers ever feel so despondent that they think suicide is their only recourse, please talk to someone, get help, stay alive. We are all better off with those we love by our side; don't let depression win. National Suicide Prevention Lifeline 1-800-273-8255.

# 14

# THE BILTMORE HOTEL

*Road trips can either suck monkey balls or, with the right person, they can be awesomesauce with cheesy fries.*
—*Penny Reid,* Friends Without Benefits

When one thinks about the Academy Awards, visions of Hollywood, Grauman's Chinese Theatre and stars laid out along a sidewalk with the names of favorite movie icons and recording stars prominently displayed on them come to mind. Downtown Los Angeles, at least for most, will be the last place one would look for Hollywood history and Academy Award fame. But here, just a couple of blocks off an old Route 66 alignment, sits one of the most historic Hollywood gathering places and at one time the largest and most luxurious hotel west of Chicago: the Los Angeles Biltmore Hotel.

Opened on October 1, 1923, the Biltmore Hotel was built with extreme luxury and allure for the wealthy in mind, showing that the city was growing up and coming of age as the entertainment capital of the world. With Hollywood and its studios in proximity to downtown Los Angeles, along with the business district in the heart of the city, the location, just off of Pershing Square and close to the proposed end of Route 66, was the obvious choice. Designing their hotel in the Art Deco style of the day, the owners spared no expense with either the exterior architecture or the interior appointments. Those entering the ornate and extravagant lobby felt as if they had just walked into one of the grand palaces of Europe rather than a hotel in the

The Millennium Biltmore still stands out as a premier hotel in downtown Los Angeles.

once sleepy city of Los Angeles. The mastermind of this opulence was Italian artist Giovanni Battista Smeraldi. Smeraldi was known for his work designing the Blue Room at the White House and many of the interiors of the Vatican. Smeraldi's work has been called "Michelangelo-esque."

It didn't take long for Hollywood and the city's elite to discover the Biltmore. The day after its opening, the hotel hosted a gala event, and more than three thousand celebrities, executives, movers and shakers were there. Clark Gable, Myrna Loy, Mary Pickford, Jack Warner and Cecil B. DeMille were all in attendance, along with a who's who of the rich and famous. The gathering was treated to a seven-course meal, drinks, dancing and a symphony that included singing canaries. The celebration was a complete success, and Hollywood was suitably impressed. The Academy of Motion Picture Arts was founded in the hotel's Crystal Ballroom in May 1927, and the Academy Awards were held in the Biltmore in 1931, 1935–39 and 1941–42. It is rumored that production designer Cedric Gibbons drew the first sketch of the Oscar award on one the hotel's linen napkins. In 1977, Bob Hope hosted the fiftieth anniversary banquet for the awards in the same room where the Academy Awards were held those many years before, the Biltmore Bowl room.

The Oscars and Hollywood parties are not the only link the Biltmore has to Tinsel Town. The hotel has had starring roles in many films and television shows since its opening. The 1939 movie *A Star Is Born*, along with *Ghostbusters*, *Bachelor Party* and *Independence Day* all use the Biltmore as a backdrop, and *The West Wing*, *That '70s Show* and, most recently, *Mad Men* have all been filmed at the Biltmore Hotel. Even Huell Howser visited here for his PBS show *Visiting*. The Biltmore Hotel may be one of the most filmed hotels in history. The first movie to use the Biltmore came less than a year after it opened when DeMille filmed *Triumph* in 1924.

It wasn't just Hollywood celebrities and film crews who visited the Biltmore, but politicians, gamblers and even mobsters frequented the speakeasy that was established at the hotel during Prohibition. When the sale and consumption of alcohol was made illegal with the passage of the Eighteenth Amendment, the Gold Room, which is adjacent to Olive Street, was converted into what can only be called a speakeasy, albeit a very proper one for the times. As respectable as the Gold Room was, it was still dealing with something that was illegal within the United States; as such, a certain element of unsavory characters came to dance and drink the night away in opulence. It is said that Al Capone, who always thought of himself merely as a businessman rather than a mobster, is said to have frequented the Biltmore.

Since alcohol was not legal and the same politicians who helped enact the amendment ignored it, along with gamblers and gangsters, a secret door leading from the Gold Room out onto Olive Street was installed for those in need of a quick getaway. The Gold Room quickly became the premier place for nightlife in Los Angeles. After Prohibition was repealed, the Biltmore still held a reputation as the "see and be seen" place to go, and it is said that Benjamin "Bugsy" Siegel frequented the hotel to wine and dine union bosses, mob moneymen and investors for his Las Vegas Casino. Today, the door leading to Olive Street is still there but now leads to a storage area, as the outer door has been bricked over.

The Biltmore Hotel was more than a refuge for the rich and famous; it was also well aware of its civic and patriotic duties. During World War II, the hotel housed servicemen as a rest station. The second floor was used for the soldiers, and those lucky enough to stay there found the contrast of life in combat compared to life here at the Biltmore striking; they thoroughly enjoyed their stay. During the war, the USO set up in the hotel and hosted charity drives, war bond events and other things needed to help the war effort. As the 1950s came and folks from all walks of life began to realize the newfound freedom of the road, travelers came to the Biltmore to celebrate in style the dawning of a new age in America. Then, in 1960, Camelot

The former lobby of the hotel is now used as a café, but the opulence is still quite visible.

had its beginnings when the Democratic National Convention was held at the Biltmore Hotel and nominated John F. Kennedy to become the next president of the United States. As people watched Kennedy accept the nomination, it seemed as if an age of idealism was dawning in America. However, as fate would have it, things didn't work out as planned.

As the 1960s came to a close, Los Angeles had become a shell of its former self. As with most big cities, Los Angeles began to see an influx of homeless. Much of this was due to its mild weather and sunshine. Shopping had shifted to areas such as Beverley Hills and the nearby beach communities, and as the city began to decline, a lawless element began to grow. As the vibrancy of the city waned, the Biltmore slowly decayed and was almost turned into a low-income retirement community. Luckily, before this could happen, an architecture firm, Ridgeway LTD, purchased the building in 1976 with the idea of restoring it to its original prominence. After an investment of about $250 million, the hotel did indeed have a revival; however, it wasn't until the Millennium & Copthorne Group purchased the hotel in 2000 that the Biltmore would see its renaissance. Today, the Millennium Biltmore Hotel is honored as an elite member of the Historic Hotels of America and once again has become one of Hollywood's swankiest hotels.

The opulence, glamour and allure of the Biltmore Hotel flourished through World War II, Korea, Vietnam, the Los Angeles riots and other national, civil and social disparity life threw at it. Gangsters, moonshiners, royalty and statesmen all passed through its doors. As of 2018, eight presidents have slept in the presidential suite: FDR, Harry Truman, JFK, LBJ, Gerald Ford, Jimmy Carter, Ronald Reagan and Bill Clinton. Celebrities and movie stars such as Joan Crawford and Dolores Del Rio, Jimmy Stewart, Clark Gable, Claudette Colbert and Ginger Rodgers, along with fashion icons like Peggy Hamilton and Hedda Hopper have all been guests at the Biltmore. One other famous personality is also known to be a frequent guest at the Millennial Biltmore, not because she was a socialite or influencer, but because the Biltmore was the last place she was seen alive and in one piece. You see, the Millennial Biltmore is said to be one of the most haunted hotels in Los Angeles.

On the morning of January 15, 1947, a woman walking with her infant along a street in Leimert Park, Los Angeles, came across what she believed to be trash dumped in an empty lot by her house. What she originally thought to be a discarded mannequin turned out to be the mutilated, bisected body of a young woman by the name of Elizabeth Short, also known as the Black Dahlia. This discovery set off one of the most famous unsolved murders

These stairs were the last place Elizabeth Short was seen alive.

in history, with a plethora of movies, books, television shows and theories that are still coming forth. What does this cold case have to do with the Millennium Biltmore Hotel? It was the last place Elizabeth Short was seen alive, and her ghost is said to walk the halls of the hotel to this day.

Elizabeth Short had been living in San Diego, California, for months before deciding to head back to Chicago to stay with her sister. Short contacted Robert Manley, a good-looking redhead from Los Angeles whom she had met at a San Diego nightclub, and asked if he would come down and drive her back to the Greyhound bus station near the Biltmore Hotel. Manley obliged. After spending the night at a Pacific Beach motel, they drove to Los Angeles, where Manley waited at the bus station while Short checked her bags and then drove the rest of the way to the Biltmore, where she said her sister was going to meet her. Short went into the hotel, had a few soft drinks and then headed upstairs; that is the last time anyone, other than her murderer, saw her alive.

There are many theories on what might have happened to Short, but I will not go into them in this narrative. If you would like the full story, read my book *Hollywood Obscura*. Regardless of what happened to this beautiful young woman, it would seem that she doesn't want to leave the lavish appointments of the Biltmore. Perhaps the most well-known sighting of the Dahlia comes from a gentleman by the name of James Moore. While staying in the hotel, Moore was heading to his room, and when he stepped into the elevator, he noticed a pretty young woman already inside. He thought this odd because the elevator had come down from the upper floors, yet the woman hadn't gotten out. As he rode up to his floor, he couldn't help but notice the woman's pale skin, accentuated by her completely black attire along with the sad look on her face. She never once spoke to him, only glancing in his direction a couple of times, never smiling. When the lift stopped at the sixth floor, the doors opened, and the woman hesitantly exited the elevator, turned to him and gave him a look conveying a feeling of helplessness and pleading that he will never forget. Before he could respond, the doors closed while he frantically pushed the button for them to reopen. Even though it took only a few seconds, when he stepped out into the hallway of the sixth floor, the woman had vanished.

A couple of days after Moore had his encounter with the young woman, he was browsing through the Last Book Store near the hotel and came across a book on true crimes and mysteries in the City of Angels. He picked the book up, and the page that it opened to had a picture of the beautiful woman he had seen in the elevator. Her name was Elizabeth Short, and she had been murdered many years previously. Moore was shocked to think that he may have taken an elevator ride with none other than the Black Dahlia herself. He knew, however, that even if it wasn't her, the woman's beauty and sadness would stay with him for the rest of his life.

Moore's story is by no means the only time someone has encountered the Dahlia. There have been numerous reports of her riding the elevator to the sixth floor, where she simply vanishes once she steps out of the car. The Black Dahlia is not the only spirit to haunt this grand hotel. Most likely due to the hotel's time as a resting place for returning military during World War II, the hotel has had many reports of ghostly soldiers passing through the old lobby. Now called the Rendezvous Court, this area serves breakfast, lunch and drinks; it is not unusual for the employees to have to field questions regarding the apparitions. Another spirit that is thought to be connected to the soldiers is that of a nurse who is commonly seen on the second floor. As this is the floor where the hotel housed the returning servicemen, one can understand where the connection might originate.

On the ninth floor, guests are often awakened in the night by the sound of a child's laughter. The laughter is that of a little girl who has been seen running and playing in the corridors, and those who have heard her giggling tell us that it sounds as if the child is having the time of her life. Many have

The Black Dahlia is frequently seen riding these elevators up to the sixth floor.

said that the sound has brought a smile to their faces from the sheer joy the child seems to be experiencing. It would seem that this young lady isn't the only child haunting the Millennium Biltmore. It is said that a young boy has been seen on the roof of the hotel. No one knows who this child is or what he is doing on the roof, and the way things are, no one ever will. When the boy is glimpsed, he has no facial features whatsoever. With no way to get an image of the boy, there is no way to discern who he might have been. Why he is on the roof is also a mystery, and he never does anything to give us a clue about his intentions.

So haunted is the Millennial Biltmore Hotel that many of the reviews left on TripAdvisor mention paranormal goings-on. One review from March 2021 stated that the room phone kept ringing but when answered would only give a dial tone. As soon as they turned around, the phone would ring again with the same result. The same person wrote that when going to sleep, they were awakened by what felt like a feather brushing their faces and they were plagued by strange dreams. Another review says that no matter where you are in the lobby or other public areas, one will feel as if they are being watched by unseen figures. Other reports from the hotel say that both employees and guests often hear the sounds of a party occurring even though there are no gatherings at the Biltmore, see apparitions out of the corner of their eyes only to find no one there when they look directly and experience sudden temperature drops, followed by noises that can't be defined.

Even though this wonderful hotel is a couple of blocks off Route 66, its luxury appointments and historic Art Deco details—along with a fairly reasonable price for what was once and still is a hotel for the rich and famous—make this a must visit for anyone who enjoys ParaTraveling. With its comfort, ambiance and a fair share of spirited activity, you do not want to miss this gem—you won't be disappointed.

# 15

# HOLLYWOOD FOREVER AND PARAMOUNT STUDIOS

*It is good to have an end to journey toward;*
*but it is the journey that matters, in the end.*
—*Ursula K. Le Guin,* The Left Hand of Darkness

Most people don't think of cemeteries when Route 66 comes to mind. They think of giant plastic statues, aging Richfield gas stations and other old, odd and strange things that have become commonplace along the Mother Road. Kitsch has become the norm and what people expect. However, Hollywood Forever Cemetery fits right in with this vision of Route 66 and is every bit as kitschy as any section of the road could want.

Founded in 1899 as the Hollywood Cemetery by a group of investors known as the Hollywood Cemetery Association on one hundred acres of land, when a section of the land was set aside for Beth Olam Cemetery, this section became the only Jewish burial ground in Hollywood and still is to this day. It is also one of the oldest cemeteries in the area. In 1939, convicted felon and millionaire Jules Roth acquired a 51 percent share in the property, and over the next sixty years Roth used cemetery funds to pay for his extreme luxurious lifestyle, while the grounds and graves of what was called Hollywood Memorial Park fell into total disrepair.

As a sad note, Jules Roth refused to allow minorities burial at the cemetery. Hattie McDaniel, the first African American to receive an Academy Award, for her portrayal of Mammy in the epic movie *Gone with the Wind*, wished to be buried in Hollywood Memorial Park, but when she passed away in 1952, she was denied by Roth. (In 1999, on the forty-seventh anniversary of McDaniel's death, the cemetery's current owner dedicated a cenotaph in her honor on the south end of the property's Sylvan Lake.)

As the headstones began to break and disappear, complaints from loved ones about those interred at the cemetery went unheeded by Roth. Instead, Roth purchased a yacht that he claimed was needed to scatter client's ashes but was used as a party boat and a place for Roth to bring the many women he cheated on his wife with for tête-à-têtes. As Roth partied and had sex, the crypts and walls of the cemetery began to crumble. At one point, an employee, fed up with Roth's inability to care for those buried at Hollywood Memorial Park, alerted

Many famous Hollywood stars are buried at Hollywood Forever.

the IRS to the embezzlement of company funds, so an investigation ensued, and Roth was forced to sell three acres of land fronting Santa Monica Boulevard (Route 66), which to this day remains a strip mall.

It all came to a head in 1974, with the cremation of Mama Cass Elliot of the group The Mamas and the Papas. The walls of the crematorium were in such bad shape that as her body was being moved into the cremator, the bricks of the furnace began to fall on and around Elliot's body. Mama Cass was eventually moved to another cemetery. Heirs of make-up artist Max Factor began complaining about damage done to his mausoleum, and many family members of those buried at the cemetery began the process of disinterment of their loved ones. By the early 1990s, the cemetery was no longer profitable, and the only money being made was the $500 charge for the removal of loved ones from the cemetery.

When Jules Roth died on January 4, 1998, an audit of the cemetery endowment fund found $9 million missing from the account, along with many other discrepancies in the accounting books. While cleaning out Roth's office, dozens of full urns were found, containing ashes that were supposed to have been scattered in the Pacific Ocean using the boat Roth had purchased for that use. Roth was originally buried in an unmarked grave, but he was later moved to a crypt in a cemetery near his parents.

In 1998, the cemetery was sold to brothers Tyler and Brent Cassidy for $375,000. The family already owned many other cemeteries in Missouri and wanted to help keep the cemetery, as well as the many famous stars buried there, from fading into obscurity. After investing millions for renovation and renaming the site Hollywood Forever, the brothers set out on a complete reimagining of what a cemetery could be. They began hosting local events, created a movie night among the tombstones, sponsored a yearly Dia de los Muertos Festival and held concerts with indie groups during the spring and summer. The only stipulation for the bands is no death metal.

With stars such as Judy Garland, Rudolph Valentino, Douglas Fairbanks, Bugsy Siegel, Johnny and Dee Dee Ramone and Looney Toons voice actor Mel Blanc, Hollywood Forever has become one of the most visited landmarks in Los Angeles. Those coming to the cemetery are here to view their idols' graves, bring flowers to their heroes and look at the magnificent artwork of headstones. Some, at least those in the know, come here to see the stars walk among the tombstones once again. For you see, this Route 66 cemetery is said to be haunted by the celebrities of the past.

A visitor at the Hollywood Forever related a tale about a strange occurrence as he tried to approach the Abbey of the Psalms mausoleum. He said that he had come celebrity grave hunting and this particular mausoleum contained quite a few stars from the past: Judy Garland, Victor Fleming, Iron Eyes Cody and Charlie Chaplin, to name a few. He said that in all other areas of the cemetery he felt nothing but peace, but as he neared the Abbey of the Psalms, a strange dread came over him. He said the closer he got to the mausoleum, the deeper the feeling became. He said that he finally had to stop and couldn't continue on into the building.

The man said he never did figure out what happened to him, why the feeling came over him, but he just felt that there was something wrong about the place, that there was something there that shouldn't have been. He felt a presence, of someone or something that shouldn't have been on hallowed ground. He didn't know if it was evil or dark, only that it wasn't supposed to be there.

This story is not unusual regarding the Abbey of the Psalms. Many people have felt that there was something in the mausoleum that shouldn't be there, and many people have also seen what it might be. Clifton Webb passed away in 1966, and he was interred in the Abbey of the Psalms. This star of *Three Coins in the Fountain*, *Mr. Belvedere Goes to College* and *Cheaper by the Dozen* may have passed, but he refuses to remain in the past.

There have been many reports of people visiting the corridor where Webb is interred who have heard whispering voices, felt unusual cold spots, witnessed strange lights and smelled Webb's signature cologne. For those who smell the cologne, the aroma is usually followed by the sight of Webb, leaning against his marker. He is always dressed in his finest suit, hat and coat, as Webb was always a stickler for looking his best, and has a kind but mischievous look and smile on his face. Webb will stare at onlookers for a few seconds, push back from the wall, tip his hat and slowly walk away from visitors until he vanishes from sight.

By his actions, Clifton Webb should not be classified as a dark or malicious entity, so it is unclear if the

Clifton Webb is seen quite often in the Abbey of the Psalms, where his body was laid in repose.

aforementioned gentleman was picking up on another spirit or perhaps just uninitiated in the ways of Psi, but when you visit the Abbey of the Psalms on your Route 66 road trip, keep an eye out for Mr. Webb and return his smile.

Virginia Rappe was not yet thirty years old when, on September 5, 1921, she attended a party at San Francisco's posh St. Francis Hotel. The party was being hosted by Roscoe "Fatty" Arbuckle. Arbuckle was one of the biggest comedic movie stars and the second-highest paid actor of the day. Rappe was engaged to be married, and she was leery of Arbuckle's reputation as a hard-drinking, partying womanizer, but she figured that the invite and exposure would be good to further her own acting career. Rappe was an established actress, but as roles for women were still hard to come by, she didn't dare let this opportunity go to waste. Arbuckle and friends Fred Fishback and Lowell Sherman bought copious amounts of bootleg booze and reserved rooms 1219, 1220 and 1221. Rappe, her friend Maude Delmont and Rappe's manager and Arbuckle's friend Al Semnacher arrived at the party just after 10:30 a.m. Not being very fond of Fatty, and hoping to ignore him as much as possible, Rappe drank numerous gin blossoms until she was quite sloshed.

By late afternoon, Virginia Rappe was feeling unwell due to the booze and asked Arbuckle if there was somewhere she could lie down. Rappe then retired to Fatty's room, 1219, and shortly afterward, Arbuckle followed and locked the door behind him. According to Maude Delmont, a little while later, she heard Virginia screaming, and when she knocked on the door, Fatty answered wearing pajamas and a robe and then flashed her a "sinister" smile. Rappe lay on the bed, writhing in agony and, when she saw Maude, called out, "He did this. He hurt me. I'm dying." After several doctors were called to the hotel, and a morphine shot failed to help, it was determined that Rappe must have internal injuries and needed surgery. The doctor figured that an external force, such as a large man lying on top of her, most likely caused a bladder rupture.

Instead of being taken to a proper hospital for surgery, hoping to cover up the illicit party, with the illegal alcohol, Rappe was brought to Wakefield Sanatorium, a maternity and abortion clinic. Over the next few days, Rappe's condition worsened, but when asked, the young woman always said that Fatty had done this to her. Virginia Rappe slipped into a coma and died on September 9, 1921.

Roscoe "Fatty" Arbuckle stood trial for the rape and murder of Rappe but, being a big-name star, was acquitted of all charges. The official cause of death was determined to be peritonitis, but questions remain regarding telltale signs of external force. Even though Arbuckle was found not guilty of all charges, his reputation was shot as far as moviegoers were concerned; the studios refused to audition him for parts and his career was over. According to William Randolph Hearst, the Arbuckle fiasco sold more papers than the sinking of the *Lusitania*. When it was all over, one of the biggest stars in Hollywood was finished, and Virginia Rappe, a rising star of the silver screen, was dead—dead, but not at rest.

Virginia Rappe is buried at Hollywood Forever Cemetery along the shore of the Sylvan Lake in the Garden of Legends. This peaceful setting has not allowed Rappe eternal rest, however. Many people have reported hearing the sound of screaming coming up from the headstone on the ground and have felt what seems to be heartbeats pulsating underneath their feet. When they place their hands on the ground where the beat is felt, the rhythm of the heart increases for a moment before finally fading away. On rare occasions, people have reported seeing a young woman, dressed in clothes from the 1920s, sitting on the edge of the lake and weeping. When they approach, the woman simply vanishes from sight. It is then that they realize the woman is sitting next to Rappe's grave.

Perhaps the most famous spirit to be seen at Hollywood Forever may also be the most recent—at least recent in her spirit form. The Cathedral Mausoleum in the southeast corner of the cemetery is where, in 1926, silent film heartthrob Rudolph Valentino was laid to rest. The year after his passing, and for the next thirty years, Ditra Flame would come to his mausoleum and leave one red rose. According to Miss Flame, the reason for her devotion stemmed from the time she was fourteen years old and deathly ill; as a favor to her mother, Valentino would go to the hospital with a single red rose and place it in her hand. He would sit by her bed to comfort her and once told her, "You're not going to die at all. You are going to live for many more years. One thing for sure, if I die before you do, please come and stay by me because I don't want to be alone." Six years later, Rudolph Valentino passed away due to complications from surgery to fix an ulcer and appendicitis. Flame never forgot his kindness or her promise.

Every year, Flame, always dressed in a black mourning dress, made the pilgrimage to place a rose on this kind man's grave. However, as Valentino's fame grew into the 1950s, the story of the "Lady in Black" leaving a rose became urban legend, and as dozens of women also dressed in black began coming to his grave every year with roses, Flame stopped showing up except for special years. Since that time, more and more women began showing up every year; there has been growing disagreement on who the original

It is said that Rappe's heartbeat can still be felt emanating from her grave.

Lady in Black, might be. There are those who say that Pola Negri, who was said to be Valentino's fiancée, was the mysterious woman; however, as we now know from actor and Valentino lover Ramon Novarro's memoirs that Valentino was gay, it is hard to believe a beard, or cover wife, would show such devotion. Over the years, many women have come forward claiming to be the mysterious Lady in Black, most too young to fit the profile and others not having a believable story. Miss Flame, however, seems to have a rock-solid basis in fact with her claims.

Ditra Flame passed away February 23, 1984, at the age of seventy-eight. Since that year, sightings of the Lady in Black have been reported every year on the anniversary of Valentino's passing. The stories are always the same. A woman, dressed in the same mourning gown Miss Flame wore, will slowly walk up to the crypt, place a single rose in the vase, stand looking at the marker before placing a kiss on her fingers, touching it to the stone and then walking away, fading from view. As the Lady in Black fades, so does the rose, until there is no sign that either had been there. It would seem, that even in death, Miss Flame keeps her promise to make sure Rudolph Valentino will never be alone.

# PARAMOUNT STUDIOS

Although not directly along Route 66, Paramount Studios sits on land that was lent and then sold to the studio by Hollywood Cemetery. Hollywood Forever Cemetery and Paramount Studios are connected by more than the land they share, since many of those who performed at the studio over the years are buried at the cemetery. They are also linked by the many spirits that come and go through the back walls of these two locations at will.

Sound stages 29–32 lie directly along the wall separating Hollywood Forever and the Paramount lot. Because of this, these stages are considered to be the most haunted spot at the studio. Footsteps are often heard in the otherwise empty stages by security as they are locking up, and equipment will often turn on without help from the living, along with cameras, lights and other needed filming equipment, which turn off on their own at the most inopportune moments during a take. Actors and crew shooting movies on these stages have often seen transparent figures wearing clothing from the 1930s and '40s that seemingly come through the back walls facing the cemetery.

Stages 31 and 32 seem to have the most activity, and many times security, making their rounds of the studio, will hear the telltale sound of the heavy sound stage doors being opened. When they go to investigate, they find that all of the doors are locked and secure. When they turn to leave, they will sometimes hear these same doors slam behind them. One story told by a couple of security guards was that one evening while securing stage 32, a third colleague left to lock up the heavy stage door, leaving the other two guards to inspect the stage and exit through the pedestrian door. As the two guards began to leave the stage, they heard someone rustling about but couldn't find anyone. Shortly after they gave up the search, they heard the large stage door being opened. Figuring it was the third security guard, they left the building, only to find their buddy waiting for them on the opposite side of the stage, near the door through which they had exited. There was no way their coworker could have opened the stage door, shut it and made it to this location in time to greet his colleagues. The third guard confirmed that he had been waiting for them for the last five minutes.

There is one location at Paramount where many guards are leery of being stationed; as such, it is usually assigned to newly hired guards or those who volunteer for the task. This location is the employee entrance gate at Lemon Grove and Van Ness Avenues. This gate and guard booth is attached to the back wall of Hollywood Forever Cemetery, and some frightening things have happened to many of the guards who work here. There have been so many reports of ghosts walking through the back wall of the cemetery that it is even getting hard to find newbies to operate the booth. One of the stranger stories that have come from this part of

Valentino may be long gone, but the Lady in Black still brings him flowers, long after her own death.

134

Paramount have to do with guards seeing heads pop through the wall from Hollywood Forever, glancing around as if looking for something or someone and then disappearing back through the solid wall. Every once in a while, a guard has told of one of these spirit's heads looking about and then staring at the guard for a few moments before disappearing back into the cemetery. A few security guards have quit their jobs rather than be posted at this gate.

Movie stars can be ego-driven and narcissistic, but many truly loved their craft and never wanted to give it up. With so many of these talented and famous stars being buried directly behind Paramount and many of those who sought their fame and fortune coming to Tinsel Town along Route 66, it should be no wonder that both Paramount Studios and the cemetery would be so haunted. After all, no one ever really wants to believe, like it says on Mel Blanc's tombstone in Hollywood Forever, "That's All Folks!"

# 16
# THE GEORGIAN HOTEL

*Happiness is planning a trip somewhere new with someone you love.*
*—unknown*

Santa Monica in the early 1900s, although known, was still considered a semi-remote location within the general Los Angeles area. Hollywood was blossoming, Los Angeles was shedding its orange grove image and this city on the coast was known for its forested coastline and pristine beaches, but not much else. All of that began to change when expensive chic hotels began to appear, along with luxurious beach clubs that offered the elite and wealthy a chance for some fun, mixed with privacy. By the 1920s, the city of Santa Monica was growing up. One of those that got in on the hotel boom was Rosamond Borde.

Rosamond was a woman before her time. Borde had the audacity to try to build a future in the male-dominated hotel industry in a time when women were meant to be seen and not heard; they were certainly not expected to compete with men in a man's field of business. Borde proved them wrong, mostly. In time, Rosamond Borde's son, Judge Harry J. Borde, decided to get into the hotel business himself. He bought a piece of land next door to his mother's hotel along Santa Monica's Ocean Avenue and began constructing the elegant Georgian Hotel. Judge Borde wanted his hotel to be an intimate hideaway catering to Los Angeles's high society and Hollywood elite, what some called Hollywood royalty. Borde knew that a posh hotel, nestled on the heavily wooded shoreline, high above the crashing waves of the Pacific

Ocean, with relatively easy access to the beaches below, could be a huge moneymaker and earn him a stellar reputation among the wealthy.

Judge Borde hired locally prominent architect Eugene Durfee to design the Georgian Hotel in the popular Art Deco style of the day. Durfee also tossed in a small touch of Romanesque Revival style for good measure. The construction began in 1931, and when the Georgian Hotel opened two years later, it was one of the first "skyscrapers" built along Ocean Avenue, remaining one of the tallest buildings in Santa Monica for many years. When opened, the hotel featured an above-street-level entrance reached by a flight of stairs, a new style for that time, balustrade balconies and differing treatments on the different stories with the lower half of the structure featuring a façade meant to look like large blocks of stone and the upper half done in flat stucco. The overall effect, combined with the Art Deco relief, was one of style and grace. Harry Brode, in honor of his mother, nicknamed the Georgian Hotel "The Lady." The hotel has sometimes been confused with the Lady Wyndemere Hotel, but they are distinctly different hotels.

Even though Prohibition was ending in 1933, when the hotel opened, the Georgian kept the speakeasy it had been constructed with just in case. This became a popular meeting place for those looking for privacy out of the public eye. Stars like Clark Gable, Charles Chaplin and Roscoe "Fatty" Arbuckle were regular guests, as were other Hollywood elites. It wasn't only the Hollywood elite who came to the Georgian Hotel for the nightlife, but some of the country's biggest names in organized crime would come here for the out-of-the-way privacy and elegance the hotel offered. Mickey Cohen, Benjamin "Bugsy" Siegel along with his girlfriend Virginia Hill and Harry "Big Greenie" Greenwood could often be found in the speakeasy. It is said that even Al "Scarface" Capone made an appearance at the Georgian Hotel. The speakeasy was becoming famous; however, it was the hotel itself that was the big draw for those coming to Santa Monica.

As Santa Monica began to grow with the defense industry coming in during the war years, the hotel saw a huge increase of guests. Many of those staying at the hotel were aircraft designers and engineers working at the growing Donald Douglas Aircraft Factory. There were others who stayed at the Georgian Hotel because of its proximity to the casino barges out in the bay and the motorboats nearby, to ferry gamblers to them. After the war, and with the new jet age emerging, the Georgian Hotel saw an increase in guests, with many jet-setting Europeans coming to California to see Hollywood and the state's legendary beaches; many sought out the Georgian Hotel as their preferred place to lay their heads. The hotel was sold in the 1950s, and the new owners set out to completely refurbish the aging Georgian Hotel.

As the 1960s dawned, the Georgian saw a resurgence of its domination as a destination hotel. However, as the world began to change with opposition to America's involvement in Vietnam, flower power and the hippie movement coming on the scene in California, the exhibition of wealth was no longer a desirable trait of society in the country. By the late 1960s, the hotel had reinvented itself as an upscale apartment building. Even though wealth was still essentially frowned upon, the Georgian's location atop the bluffs directly overlooking the Pacific Ocean was still prime real estate that demanded an exclusive residency. Perhaps the most esteemed tenant to stay at the apartments was none other than Kennedy matriarch, philanthropist and socialite Rose Kennedy. Rose would spend her summers at the Georgian entertaining Hollywood's prominent film directors, movie stars, business executives and journalists out front on the hotel's oceanfront veranda. She was not by any means the only mover and shaker to reside at this spectacular apartment building.

The apartments were finally reconverted into hotel rooms in the 1990s, and in the spring of 2000, an extensive $2 million restoration of the property was completed. The guest rooms were upgraded with new, modern, elegant amenities, the lobby was improved along with meeting facilities, and even the hallways themselves were upgraded. All in all, the new Georgian Hotel perfectly combines the stylish elements of the past and those of the modern into a grand spectacle. As the hotel reemerged, so too did the clientele of Hollywood. It is not uncommon to see stars such as Robert Downey Jr., Al Pacino, Nicolas Cage, Britney Spears and others frequenting the hotel basement bar. It seems that the old hotel has come full circle and is once again the location for movers and shakers around the globe.

Even though the Georgian Hotel is not actually on Route 66, nor has it ever been, its location at the end of Santa Monica Boulevard has garnered it a place within the road's ethos. Route 66 turns south off Santa Monica Boulevard onto Lincoln Boulevard and then continues only a mile to the terminus at Olympic Boulevard. Santa Monica Boulevard continues another mile and a half past Lincoln before dead ending at Ocean Avenue. The reason for the confusion of so many believing that Route 66 continued on is due to the fact that many traveling along the Mother Road, seeing the vast Pacific Ocean, continued down Santa Monica Boulevard until they reached the coast, where they inevitably saw the pier and then continued on to explore that venue. Today, Ocean Avenue and Santa Monica Boulevard

The Georgian Hotel stands out as perhaps the most historic hotel in all of Santa Monica.

enjoy the title of the "Spiritual End" of Route 66. There is a plaque overlooking the ocean announcing the end of the Will Rodgers Highway. No matter what "end" of the Mother Road at which one finds themselves, the Georgian Hotel, at the "spiritual end" of Route 66, has its own spirits that have remained to enjoy the hotel even after death.

Over the years, the Georgian Hotel has built a reputation as not only one of the premier hotels in Los Angeles but also a location with ghostly occurrences. Most of these stories come from the area where the old speakeasy was located. It is not hard to believe, since the area was where people gathered for a good time and was where some of the most notorious gangsters in American history came to enjoy drinks and perhaps conduct under-the-table business dealings. Some of the reports that have come from this area are the sounds of gasping and sighs coming from empty tables and the phantom footsteps in the otherwise empty room. Many employees also say that on quite a few occasions, as they walk into the room, they will hear a voice call out with a cheerful, "Good morning." Many of the newer employees have said that this spirit seems to want to get to know the employees before greeting them, as it has taken awhile for them to hear the greeting themselves.

In this same area of the hotel, it is not unusual for guests to see wispy figures sitting at otherwise empty tables, and these apparitions have also been seen walking around the room and both entering and leaving through the doors of the old speakeasy. It has been said that Benjamin "Bugsy" Siegel has been seen sitting at a table from time to time. Every time this sighting has been reported, it is always the same table in the restaurant, and those reporting the manifestation say that the apparition is only seen for a moment before fading from view. Some claim that Siegel will flash them his trademark smile before vanishing. Why Bugsy would be haunting the Georgian Hotel is a mystery; however, Bugsy is known for his pleasantness toward strangers in his haunts at the Flamingo Hotel in Las Vegas.

Many of the staff working at the restaurant now housed within the old speakeasy have reported strange things happening in the kitchens. There are reports of pots and pans mysteriously dropping from their storage racks, utensils turning up missing, only to be found later right where they were supposed to be, along with cans, seasonings and other foodstuffs being rearranged for no discernable reason or any employee admitting to doing it. With so much going on within the hotel's restaurant, it is not hard to believe that things also go on in other parts of the hotel.

The *Santa Monica Daily Press* wrote an article stating that "some current guests allege the spirits of former tenants still linger." It can be assumed that, even though the Georgian had a short duration as an apartment building, those who were lucky enough to live in a place with such a magnificent view as the Georgian might not want to leave after they passed away. Many of these spirits may be confused as to why so many unknown folks come to sleep in their "apartments," or they may simply like to play with the living. Whatever the case may be, even the staff at the hotel have reported odd things going on in the upper floors. Front desk clerks have said they will receive calls from empty rooms, have room service meals requested to be sent to rooms that are unoccupied and have to make up rooms that hadn't seen guests in days. There have even been times housekeeping has heard the sound of muted conversations coming from otherwise vacant rooms.

The *Santa Monica Daily Press* story continued, "One of our overnight officers tells a story about getting a telephone call from a guest room that was not occupied and just heard giggling." Another report told to the paper said that "a guest claims to have checked into their room, put their stuff down and jumped into the shower. When they came out the television was on, the bed was open and the suitcase was empty." One can even find reviews of the hotel online where guests have commented about activity that they experienced while staying at the Georgian Hotel.

Even though the Georgian Hotel is not on the Mother Road, per se, it is at one of those ends that people associate with Route 66. Regardless, the Georgian Hotel is a spectacular remnant of what old Route 66 was meant to be. Although a bit pricey, a stay at this wonderfully luxurious hotel is well worth it. For those looking to stay at a truly haunted inn, the Georgian Hotel should be near the top of the list for any ParaTraveler visiting California and driving down the state's haunted Route 66.

# 17

# THE SANTA MONICA PIER

*It's always best to start at the beginning—and all you do is follow
the Yellow Brick Road.*
*—Glinda, the Good Witch of the North, from* The Wizard of Oz

The Santa Monica Pier is another one of the Route 66 end points
that actually have no basis in Mother Road history, although many
would disagree. Like the intersection of Santa Monica Boulevard
and Ocean Avenue, the pier is not the western terminus of Route 66 but the
newest of the "end points." Most people believe the pier to be the end of the
trail due to excellent marketing between a Route 66 souvenir shop, the Route
66 Alliance and the Pier Restoration Corporation. This took place in 2009
when the city "dedicated" the pier as "the end of the trail." The dedication
coincided with the opening of the souvenir shop, and the unofficial terminus
of the Mother Road was forever changed in the minds of travelers.

The Santa Monica Pier had humble origins rooted in the need for sewage
disposal. In 1909, the city, needing a way to dispose of the waste, decided
that a 1,600-foot-long municipal pier with a pipeline running under it would
be the perfect solution to get rid of the treated sewage—sending it out into
the bay. Luckily for visitors to the pier, and the bay itself, this lasted only
until the 1920s. Regardless of the true purpose of the pier, opening day saw
thousands of people come to see the new pier, the navy cruiser USS *Albany*
and the many performers who were there to entertain. The Santa Monica
Pier became an instant favorite among the fishermen in the community, and

The yacht harbor sign at the Santa Monica Pier has become so famous that it has become a symbol of California's sunshine and beaches for folks all around the world.

with the vast number of fish in the bay at that time, no one would go hungry while people could drop their line from the pier.

Although fishing was becoming the main use for the pier, folks were always hoping to have an amusement pier like those on the Atlantic coast and one that could compete with Ocean Park and the pier in neighboring Venice, California. Charles Looff, a famous carousel carver and amusement entrepreneur, seeing an opportunity, convinced the city to allow him to build a wider pier, replete with an amusement park along the south side of the existing pier. The new Looff Pleasure Pier opened on June 12, 1916, with a bowling and billiards building, a fun house called What Is It and the Blue Streak Racer roller coaster. By far the most popular attraction at the new amusement pier was the Looff Hippodrome and its brand-new carousel. The Looff carousel featured an extra row of horses on one of the finest rides of its kind in the country. With live music, a picnic pavilion, fishing and entertainment, the pier became a prime destination for locals and tourists alike.

U.S. Navy warships would visit the pier on a regular basis during the early days, and folks would flock to see them. During a visit of the battleship *Texas* (BB-35) and the auxiliary cruiser USS *Prairie*, so many people crowded onto the west end of the pier that the concrete gave way and dropped two feet, causing panic among the guests. Concrete was still new at the time, and rust had caused the material to weaken and fail with the weight of the crowd. The pier and the pilings were rebuilt using creosote-treated wood. So new was this method of using creosote that the pier was featured in the magazine *Popular Mechanics*. It took two years to complete the repairs; by then, 1924, Looff had passed away, and his son, busy with the other parks in their portfolio, sold the Santa Monica Pier to a local enterprise, the Santa Monica Amusement Company.

One of the first things the group did was to remove the old coaster and replace it with the new Whirlwind Dipper. This was a bigger version of the Giant Dipper roller coasters at Belmont Park, in San Diego, and the one on the Santa Cruz Boardwalk in Northern California. Another addition was the La Monica Ballroom. The ballroom opened on July 23, 1924, and over fifty thousand people showed up to see this fifteen-thousand-square-foot, hard maple dance floor and "submarine garden," in the largest ballroom in the world. Opening day of the La Monica marked the first traffic jam in Santa Monica history. The ballroom, and the pier itself, had entered a period of prosperity and notoriety. Unfortunately, this was not to last, and when the Depression hit, the pier became, in essence, a ghost town.

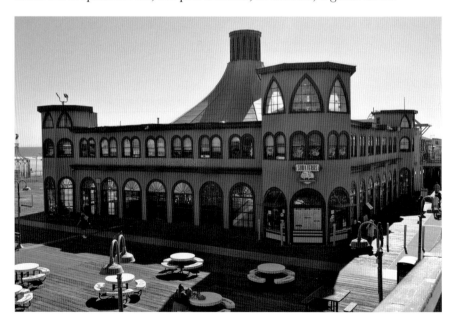

The Looff Hippodrome is still a favorite for families and tourists alike even after one hundred years.

During the Depression days, the pleasure pier was all but abandoned. By 1930, all of the rides but the carousel had been removed, and the La Monica, its dance floor no longer needed, became a convention center, a lifeguard headquarters and, for a short time, part of the city jail. The municipal pier, still a popular fishing spot, became crowded with people fishing just so they didn't starve to death. One man, who had come to Santa Monica for his retirement, upon seeing the pier, "unretired" and started his own for-hire fishing fleet in 1925. By the time the Great Depression was in full swing, he had made enough money that he was able to help folks by donating a portion of his own catch to needy families in the area. He was also instrumental in helping keep commercial fishing out of the Santa Monica Bay and was always involved with other community concerns. In 1929, E.C. Segar premiered his new comic strip, *Popeye*, at the Thimble Theater. Segar, who was a regular visitor to the Santa Monica Pier, had gotten the idea for his hero from this fisherman, Olaf C. Olsen, and his many good works.

Even with the Depression in full swing, there were still wealthy Americans who demanded their luxuries. The pier had always drawn the boating community, and now the yachting crowd wanted more from the city. In 1933, a bond was issued to construct a breakwater and create a yacht harbor. This became a public works project, which allowed many men to have a job that they might not have had during this time. When the 3,200-foot-long causeway was completed in July 1934, the city celebrated by holding the Santa Monica Regatta. Moorings for the new yacht harbor were highly sought after, and one of the first to buy a slip was none other than Charlie Chaplin. Other Hollywood stars soon followed; in 1941, a new bridge to the pier and harbor was constructed. Not long after, the businesses got together and installed a big, blue, arched, sign reading, "Santa Monica Yacht Harbor." That sign has since become the internationally known symbol of the pier and Santa Monica itself.

During the Depression, gambling was still a pastime for many folks, and the mob was happy to help. In 1938, Tony "The Hat" Cornero set up a gambling barge, the SS *Rex*, three miles offshore, and used the pier as the base for the mob's water taxi service. As happens when booze and gambling mix, this began to cause a problem on the pier and for the city. The city fought Cornero, but it took District Attorney Earl Warren to come up with the solution to the problem; he declared the legal distance for gambling ships to be several more miles offshore. This made the entire venture untenable for water taxis. The mob refused to move the SS *Rex*, and an eight-day standoff occurred when the mobsters used high-power water hoses to hold off authorities, but The Hat finally gave up, saying he needed a haircut.

During World War II, the U.S. Navy assumed control over all of California's large harbors; as such, commercial fishing boats had nowhere to dock and offload their catch. As Santa Monica was the only place for them to go, they began unloading at the pier. Large trucks would come, pick up the seafood and haul it off to be used by the military and civilians alike. As the pier was not designed for this, by 1942, the pier's structure was beginning to deteriorate. Not wanting the pier to collapse, officials began refusing to allow the boats to deliver their catch. In revolt, the fishing boats dumped their haul into the bay, causing the water to become polluted. It took the government in Washington to agree to fortify the pier before deliveries were again accepted.

In 1943, local banker Walter Newcomb bought the lease from Santa Monica Amusement Company in the belief that once the war ended, people would again come back to the pier. When the war ended, folks did indeed come back. He immediately began adding rides back to the boardwalk and replaced the original Looff carousel in 1947 with the 1922 Philadelphia Toboggan Company one he already owned. Newcomb died in 1948, and his wife took over the company. The pier was able to continue its tourist trade, but as age caught up with the structure, upkeep became quite expensive and began eating up profits. The pier began to decline. By the 1960s, with the lease set to expire in 1974, the Newcombs told the city they would not renew the lease when the time came. With both the Pleasure Pier and Municipal Pier being in such bad shape, along with the entire area being dubbed "seedy" and an "eyesore," the city mulled over what should be done with it. While the city tried to make up its mind, the pier began to attract activists such as Tom Hayden, Jane Fonda and Charles Bukowski. People began living in apartments that were once offices in several of the buildings, including the "Merry Go-Round" building, otherwise known as the Looff Hippodrome, and the pier became a community in its own right.

In 1972, the City of Santa Monica had finally made up its mind on what to do with the pier. During a council meeting, it was decided that the entire thing would be demolished. With the decision made, the community rose up in revolt. So strong was the opposition that the city council was forced to rescind its decision. In a testament to how strongly the citizens of Santa Monica felt about the pier, not a single council member who voted for demolition, regardless of whether or not they voted to rescind,

The carousel inside the Looff Hippodrome is said to be a favorite of Norma Jean Baker and an unknown dark rider.

was reelected or ever held office in the city again. In 1975, and with overwhelming support, Santa Monica's Proposition 1 was voted in, which preserves the pier forever.

Today, the Santa Monica Pier is the most visited location in the city for both locals and tourists. It has become a destination for folks from all over the country and the world. The Looff Hippodrome is still there, and once again the carousel is one of the biggest attractions of the many that now grace the boardwalk. With a roller coaster, the Sea Dragon swing ride, food and fun for all ages, the pier has something for everyone. The Santa Monica Pier has the distinction of being the only amusement pier left in California, and it is still free for people to walk among the historic buildings and walkways. The pier has been added to the National Register of Historic Places so future generations, along with folks long past life, can still enjoy this fun and safe attraction. Over the years, the Santa Monica Pier has had strange tales told about ghosts, and shadows wandering its buildings, rides, and rooftops. One of the most prominent locations for these odd goings-on is none other than the Looff Hippodrome.

During the 1960s, the office space on the second floor of the hippodrome was converted into apartments. As folks do, many of the residents would hold parties and gatherings for friends, and many of these would go late into the night. Residents, trying to clean up well into the early morning hours, would claim to hear footsteps coming down the hallways toward them. Thinking it was one of their guests coming back after forgetting something, they would step out into the hall to greet them and find that there was no one there even though the footsteps could still be heard. Guests would call their host days after the gathering and tell them how they had felt someone watching them as they walked down the hall, and many claimed to hear these same phantom footfalls as if someone were following them out. They would go on to say that even though they could hear the footsteps, they never saw who, or what, was causing them.

Residents would often tell of hearing the sound of calliope music coming up from the carousel below them. They would quickly run downstairs to see if someone had gotten into the control room and somehow gotten the non-functioning ride started up, but no one was ever found, and nobody ever figured out how the music could play from the ride while shut down. The calliope music became so frequent that folks living here began to realize that it must be spirits still coming to the pier to enjoy themselves. Many found it almost comforting as they figured it meant the spirits were happy. This music is still heard to this day, late at night and early in the morning. As the apartments burned down in 1975 and were then converted into government offices once again, the reports of these footsteps and hearing the calliope music have lessened considerably. However, the music is still heard often by employees, and visitors during the evening hours.

One spirit that has been seen at the hippodrome has been seen so often that it has become an urban legend among folks who know the pier. Visitors and employees alike have seen a shadowy figure walking along the rooftop of the hippodrome. This figure is said to be all black and at times appears to be wispy, as if made of smoke or vapor, although at other times the spirit is solid. This apparition is not relegated solely to the roof of the hippodrome but has also been seen on other roofs of the pier. No one knows who this ghost may be, and some speculate that he is a quintessential shadow being; however, this spirit seems to differ from other shadow figures. The main difference has to do with the fact that this entity has been seen riding on the carousel horses. Many folks visiting the pier late at night have said that they have seen this specter on various horses, riding along with other guests just as if he is one of them. At other times he will appear completely alone on the carousel. Witnessing this specter is not dependent on time of day, as he is seen at all hours of the day and night.

There is another spirit that is said to haunt the hippodrome, and this one is anything but scary or harmful. In fact, from the way this ghost lived, the best word to describe her would be *sad*. Marilyn Monroe is said to haunt a few places, some that were important to her in life: the home where she died; the Hollywood Roosevelt Hotel, where she lived for a time; and the Santa Monica Pier. Marilyn Monroe would come to the pier, in disguise, in the hopes that she could regain just a bit of the woman she had been. Norma Jean Baker loved amusement parks, and growing up nearby, she would come to the pier as a young woman to ride the carousel. After becoming a big-name star, having her name changed and the studios getting and keeping her hooked on Nembutal, Norma Jean would come to the pier just to sit in contemplation, ride the carousel as she did in her younger days and hope she could stop being Marilyn Monroe for just a little bit. It is said that if you are in the hippodrome late at night and watch the mirrors as they spin around, you can sometimes catch a glimpse of her sitting on her favorite bench near the giftshop. As with the mirror that once graced her room while living at the Roosevelt, once you turn away from the glass to get an unobstructed

The Sea Dragon ride is said to have a phantom rider, much like the spirit who enjoys the carousel.

view of this beautiful lady, she will have disappeared from sight, only to reappear once you glance back to the carousel mirrors.

There have been many reports from the employees who work on the pier of hearing footsteps following them as they make their way from their shop to their cars, but never have they seen who is following them. At other times, these same employees have seen strange shadows walking along the end of the pier and among the many buildings that stretch out along its length. It is believed these figures could be the spirits of those who died on the pier from accidents, suicide or the many murders and mob activities that had plagued the pier in its past. There have even been reports of folks seeing a strange wispy figure riding the giant, swinging ship known as the Sea Dragon. This rider, as with the spirit riding the carousel, is sometimes seen among the living riders and at other times far away from them. Some believe this spirit to be the same one as on the carousel. If this is the case, he too goes against the shadow person theory. Unfortunately, no one knows for sure.

There is more to the Santa Monica Pier than meets the eye. It has a long and storied history, from Santa Monica Pier lifeguard Preston Peterson's invention of a device still used to save lives today, the "Peterson Tube," to spreading the Hawaiian sport of paddle boarding around the country and the world by holding races in the 1950s, the pier has had a profound impact on water sports. Toss in the offshore gambling limit, introduction of now widely used construction materials and the early beginnings of the Heal the Bay movement, Santa Monica and its Pleasure Pier have had a direct impact on the world in general.

The pier is still a great place to take the family for a day at the beach, an original Hot Dog on a Stick and some fun amusement park rides. Fun, sun, food and history, who could really ask for more? Maybe that is the reason so many are still coming back, even in death.

# EPILOGUE

*You never know the value of a moment until it becomes a memory.*
*—Dr. Seuss*

The Mother Road has become a piece of American lore that has spread to all parts of the globe. Folks come from all over the world to travel this enthralling roadway and marvel at the architecture of old, the kitsch that delights us today and the promise of tomorrow that still lives on Route 66. Tours are held annually that span a single state and region, and others that take you the entire distance start to finish, in vintage automobiles, on motorcycles or just in your modern family car. What was once simply a road taking you from point A to B, or as a path to a new life, has become both a tourist highway and a retail opportunity catering to folks' desire for a slower life and simpler times. This commercialism, although bringing many towns and burgs back to life and keeping others alive, has sometimes caused friction between the Mother Road puritans and those who think of Route 66 simply as entertainment.

One of the biggest bones of contention has brewed up in California at the end of the route. What should be the culmination of a fun road trip can turn into an argument over which end one picks for their journey's end. You see, there are three "ends" in California, more if you count past alignments, and folks can never seem to agree on which is the true end. When folks originally drove the route, they just kept going until they saw the ocean; today, there is a plaque and sign stating that spot is the end of Route 66, known as the end

*Above*: The official end of Route 66 is at the intersection of Lincoln and Olympic Boulevards, with only a small sign to mark the end of an epic journey.

*Left*: The "End of the Trail" sign at the Santa Monica Pier has become the most photographed sign for the end of the Mother Road, even though it is blocks away from the true end.

This sign at the intersection of Santa Monica Boulevard and Ocean Avenue claims to be the "West End of Route 66," yet it is more than a mile away from the official end of the Mother Road.

of the "Will Rogers Highway." Although a mile away from the actual end of the highway, this has come to be known as the "spiritual end" of Route 66. Another end has actually only been in existence since 2009, that of the Santa Monica Pier; although actually a few blocks away from the official end, it has come to be known as the "symbolic end" of Route 66. The actual, official end of the Mother Road sits unobtrusively at the intersection of Lincoln and Olympic Boulevards. With only a small sign, set high on a light pole, it is not hard to understand the confusion, as the other "end" signs are prominently displayed for all to see.

There is no right or wrong in which end point one choses as the terminus, and the arguments are a show of uselessness. What is important is not the end but the journey. I would say that for the road tripper, a visit to all three would make it the best end of all. That way, when one harkens back, the ParaTraveler can truly say they saw it all and visited with many folks, both living and dead, for the best haunted road trip of their lives.

# BIBLIOGRAPHY

## BOOKS

Clune, Brian. *Hollywood Obscura*. Atglen, PA: Schiffer Books, 2017.
Clune, Brian, and Bob Davis. *Ghosts and Legends of Calico*. Charleston, SC: The History Press, 2020.


## AMBOY

Abandoned Places. "Amboy California Ghost Town on Route 66." https://abandonedway.com.
The Place of Scary—Haunted Places. "Amboy School—Amboy, California." https://hauntedplacesofusa.blogspot.com.


## AZTEC HOTEL

Atomic Redhead. "A Look Inside the Strange and Haunted Aztec Hotel of Route 66." July 1, 2021. https://atomicredhead.com.
Evains, Tyler Shaun. "Will the Aztec Hotel in Monrovia Finally Reopen? It's Getting Closer, Here's the Latest." *San Gabriel Valley Tribune*, March 19, 2019. https://www.sgvtribune.com.
Rasmussen, Cecilia. "Maya Landmark on Route 66 Became Haunt of Actors, Ghosts." *Los Angeles Times*, March 25, 2001. https://www.latimes.com.

## COLORADO STREET (SUICIDE) BRIDGE

Legends of America. "Suicide Bridge—Colorado Street Bridge in Pasadena, California." https://www.legendsofamerica.com.

Masters, Nathan. "Colorado Street Bridge: The Birth of a Pasadena Landmark." KCET, November 22, 2013. https://www.kcet.org.

Monroe, Heather. "The History of Pasadena's Haunted Suicide Bridge." January 15, 2021. https://heathermonroe.medium.com.

## THE GEORGIAN HOTEL

The Georgian. "Santa Monica's First Lady." https://www.georgianhotel.com.

Legends of America. "The Haunted Georgian Hotel, Santa Monica, California." https://www.legendsofamerica.com.

Santa Monica. "Stories of Santa Monica's Haunted Past." October 30, 2017. https://www.santamonica.com.

## GOFFS

Digital Desert. "History of Goffs." https://digital-desert.com.

## HARVEY HOUSE

Haunted Houses. "Casa de Desierto Harvey House Museum." https://hauntedhouses.com.

Kansapedia. "Fred Harvey." https://www.kshs.org.

## HISTORY

California Historic Route 66 Association. "About Us." https://www.route66ca.org.

National Center for Preservation Technology and Training. "Special Resource Study: Route 66." https://ncptt.nps.gov.

National Park Service. "Route 66 Overview." https://www.nps.gov.

Route 66. "Historic Route 66 in California." https://www.route66guide.com.

## HOLLYWOOD FOREVER AND PARAMOUNT

Hollywood Forever. https://hollywoodforever.com.
Kantor, Loren. "The Strange History of Hollywood Forever Cemetery." *Medium*, July 22, 2020. https://medium.com.
LA Ghosts. "Hollywood Forever Cemetery." https://laghosttour.com.
Our Haunted Spaces. "Haunted Paramount Studios." https://ourhauntedspaces.wordpress.com.


## LUDLOW

Hall, Sharon. "Route 66 Ghost Towns: Ludlow, California." *Digging History*, December 18, 2013. https://digging-history.com.


## MILLENNIUM BILTMORE HOTEL

Truhley, Kimberley. "The Millennium Biltmore Hotel: The Story of an LA Icon." Discover Los Angeles, March 25, 2021. https://www.discoverlosangeles.com.
Van Winkle, Claire. "The Millennium Biltmore Hotel: Everyone from Al Capone to John F. Kennedy Has Spent the Night." Storied Hotels, October 8, 2018. https://storiedhotels.com.
The Scare Chamber. "The Haunted Millennium Biltmore Hotel." https://www.thescarechamber.com.


## ORO GRANDE

Learn Religions. "Bottle Trees." https://www.learnreligions.com.
Roadside America. "Elmer Long's Bottle Tree Ranch." https://www.roadsideamerica.com.
The Route-66. "About Oro Grande California." https://www.theroute-66.com.
Thompson, Richard D. "Sagebrush Anne and the Sagebrush Route." http://members.uia.net/richkat/sagebrush1.html.

## PASADENA PLAYHOUSE

Paranormal Housewives. "Haunted Pasadena Playhouse." https://paranormalhousewives.wordpress.com.

Pasadena, California. "Pasadena Playhouse." https://www.visitpasadena.com.

U-S-History.com "Pasadena Playhouse." https://www.u-s-history.com.

Waymarking. "The Pasadena Playhouse." https://www.waymarking.com.


## SANTA MONICA PIER

Santa Monia Pier. "Our Storied Past." https://www.santamonicapier.org.

Trujillo, Jovita. "Celebrity Ghosts and the Places They've Been Seen." Hola! October 18, 2021. https://www.hola.com.

# ABOUT THE AUTHOR

Brian Clune is the co-founder and the historian for Planet Paranormal Radio and Planet Paranormal Investigations. He has traveled the entire state of California researching its haunted hot spots and historical locations in an effort to bring knowledge of the paranormal and the wonderful history of the state to those interested in learning.

His interest in history has led him to volunteer aboard the USS *Iowa* and the Fort MacArthur Military Museum as well as giving lectures and classes at colleges and universities around the state. He has been involved with numerous TV shows, including *Ghost Adventures*, *My Ghost Story*, *Dead Files* and *Ghost Hunters* and was the subject in a companion documentary for the movie *Paranormal Asylum*. He has also appeared on numerous local and national and international radio programs. Clune is the co-host for the radio program *The Full Spectrum Project*, which deals in subjects ranging from ghosts and murders to all things odd and weird both natural and supernatural.

His other books include *California's Historic Haunts*, published by Schiffer Books, and the highly acclaimed *Ghosts of the Queen Mary*, published by The History Press, as well as *Ghosts and Legends of Alcatraz* and *Ghosts and Legends of Calico*, all with coauthor Bob Davis. Brian and Bob also teamed up to write the riveting biography of Ghost Box creator Frank Sumption. Clune is also the author of *Haunted San Pedro* and *Hollywood Obscura*, the spellbinding book dealing with Hollywood's dark and sordid tales of murder and ghosts. Clune is currently working on other titles for The History Press and is teaching courses in paranormal studies at California State University Dominguez Hills.

Clune lives in Southern California with his loving wife, Terri, his three wonderful children and of course, Wandering Wyatt!

OTHER BOOKS BY BRIAN CLUNE

*Ghosts of the Queen Mary* (The History Press, 2014)

*California's Historic Haunts* (Schiffer Books, 2015)

*Haunted San Pedro* (The History Press, 2016)

*Hollywood Obscura: Death, Murder and the Paranormal Aftermath*
(Schiffer Books, 2017)

*Haunted Universal Studios* (The History Press, 2018)

*Ghosts and Legends of Alcatraz* (The History Press, 2019)

*Thinking Outside the Box: Frank Sumption, Creator of the Ghost Box*
(Palmetto Publishing, 2019)

*Ghosts and Legends of Calico* (The History Press, 2020)

*Haunted Heart of San Diego* (The History Press, 2021)

*Legends and Lore Along California's Highway 395* (The History Press, 2022)

*Haunted Southern California* (The History Press, 2022)

*Dark Tourism: California* (Schiffer Books, scheduled for release May 2022)

Brian Clune and his book *Ghosts of the Queen Mary* were featured in
*LIFE Magazine: Worlds Most Haunted Places: Creepy, Ghostly and Notorious Spots*
(LIFE, 2018)